Contents

Terrorism and America

WITHDRAWN

BCSIA Studies in International Security
Belfer Center for Science and International Affairs (BCSIA)
John F. Kennedy School of Government, Harvard University

Michael E. Brown, Sean M. Lynn-Jones, and Steven E. Miller, series editors
Karen Motley, executive editor

Allison, Graham T., Owen R. Coté, Jr., Richard A. Falkenrath, and Steven E. Miller, *Avoiding Nuclear Anarchy: Containing the Threat of Loose Russian Nuclear Weapons and Fissile Material* (1996)

Allison, Graham T., and Kalypso Nicolaïdis, eds., *The Greek Paradox: Promise vs. Performance* (1996)

Arbatov, Alexei, Abram Chayes, Antonia Handler Chayes, and Lara Olson, eds., *Managing Conflict in the Former Soviet Union: Russian and American Perspectives* (1997)

Bennett, Andrew, *Condemned to Repetition? The Rise, Fall, and Reprise of Soviet-Russian Military Interventionism, 1973–1996* (1999)

Blackwill, Robert D., and Michael Sturmer, eds., *Allies Divided: Transatlantic Policies for the Greater Middle East* (1997)

Brom, Shlomo, and Yiftah Shapir, eds., *The Middle East Military Balance, 1999–2000* (1999)

Brown, Michael E., ed., *The International Dimensions of Internal Conflict* (1996)

Brown, Michael E., and Sumit Ganguly, eds., *Government Policies and Ethnic Relations in Asia and the Pacific* (1997)

Elman, Miriam Fendius, ed., *Paths to Peace: Is Democracy the Answer?* (1997)

Falkenrath, Richard A., *Shaping Europe's Military Order: The Origins and Consequences of the CFE Treaty* (1994)

Falkenrath, Richard A., Robert D. Newman, and Bradley A. Thayer, *America's Achilles' Heel: Nuclear, Biological, and Chemical Terrorism and Covert Attack* (1998)

Feldman, Shai, *Nuclear Weapons and Arms Control in the Middle East* (1996)

Forsberg, Randall, ed., *The Arms Production Dilemma: Contraction and Restraint in the World Combat Aircraft Industry* (1994)

Hagerty, Devin T., *The Consequences of Nuclear Proliferation: Lessons from South Asia* (1998)

Kokoshin, Andrei A., *Soviet Strategic Thought, 1917-91* (1998)

Lederberg, Joshua, *Biological Weapons: Limiting the Threat* (1999)

Shields, John M., and William C. Potter, eds., *Dismantling the Cold War: U.S. and NIS Perspectives on the Nunn-Lugar Cooperative Threat Reduction Program* (1997)

Terrorism and America

A Commonsense Strategy for a Democratic Society

Philip B. Heymann

The MIT Press
Cambridge, Massachusetts
London, England

Second printing, 2001
First MIT Press paperback edition, 2000
©1998 by Philip B. Heymann

Library of Congress Cataloging-in-Publication Data

Heymann, Philip B.
Terrorism and America : a commonsense strategy for a democratic society / Philip B. Heymann.
p.   cm. — (BCSIA studies in international security)
Includes bibliographical references (p.   ) and index.
ISBN 0-262-08272-1 (hc : alk. paper), 0-262-58197-3 (pb)
1. Terrorism—United States. 2. Terrorism—United States—Prevention. I. Belfer Center for Science and International Affairs. II. Title. III. Series.
HV6432.H49   1998
363.3'2'0973—dc21   98-4073
                                                     CIP

Acknowledgments

This book is very much the fruit of five years of working together with two colleagues whose ideas and learning are in every chapter. Dr. Ariel Merari of the University of Tel Aviv has advised Israel and often the United States on every aspect of dealing with terrorism. Our mutual friend and colleague Dr. Daniel McGillis taught at Harvard Law School with us for five years, educated us on Northern Ireland, and contributed constantly to our joint exploration, leading to this volume. I am greatly indebted to both friends. That joint effort and this book would not have been possible without a very generous grant from the John D. and Catherine T. MacArthur Foundation.

That I wrote and rewrote this material until it took its present form is the result of the insistence and help of my dearest friend, Ann Heymann.

Producing the manuscript depended on the skills, work, and constant good humor of my assistant, Jody Clineff.

Preface to the Paperback Edition

The broadest message of this book is that terrorism invites disproportionate fear and disproportionate demands for stern governmental responses, whether or not they are useful. As its subtitle indicates,
the book is a call for the use of informed and thoughtful common
sense. Nothing in the terrible losses—223 dead and 4,800 injured—
from the almost simultaneous bombings of the U.S. embassies in
Nairobi, Kenya and Dar es Salaam, Tanzania changes that prescription.

For more than a century, terrorism has relied almost exclusively
on three by now familiar tactics. Since the invention of dynamite, it
has used bombings and explosions. The car bombs used against the
embassies, at the World Trade Center, and in Oklahoma City were
conventional explosives with unusually great destructive capacities.
Assassinations of political leaders have been a second major device.
Finally, terrorists have taken hostages, often by hijacking planes.
Still, the overall pattern is one of limited force used for its psychological and political impact. From the point of view of threatened governments there have been two tasks: first, to try to prevent the terrorist
event from taking place; and, second, if prevention fails, to deal with
the after-effects or consequences, including the remarkably large
political effect of acts of terrorism.

If anything has changed in the two years since this book was first
published, it is the heightening of concern that terrorism may move
from a tactic causing relatively few deaths and relatively little other

destruction, despite immense public concern, to a phenomenon where weapons of mass destruction may become terrorist tools. The particular weapons that are feared are nuclear and biological. If actually used, the death toll on a single occasion could easily be thousands of times the annual deaths in recent years from terrorism in the United States.

No one can measure the risk of such a terrorist event. So far very few such events have been attempted, a fact that suggests either unusual practical difficulties in acquiring and using either type of weapon, or substantial moral and political inhibitions to such escalation by terrorist groups. In short, nuclear or biological terrorism would require both unusual technical capabilities and a desire to do damage that very few terrorists have yet displayed. (Even as to far-less-difficult terrorism with chemical weapons, the list of organizations that have developed that capability is short—perhaps including Aum Shinrikyo, Hamas, and the group led by Osama bin Laden.)

Obtaining the enriched uranium or plutonium necessary for a nuclear bomb is no easy task, despite our fears of weakened security arrangements in the aftermath of the collapse of the Soviet Union. The required delivery system for a biological weapon generally involves reducing anthrax or another organism to a size that allows it to operate as a floating aerosol and, in the case of anthrax, to reach the lungs. Accomplishing this is fortunately a substantial technological feat.

Still, the risk of terrorist use of nuclear or biological weapons, however small, has come to dominate the perceived dangers to the United States in a time without great foreign challenges. And the needed skills and will might both be provided by one of the small-to-medium-sized nations that are extremely hostile to the United States.

Implications for Deterrence, Prevention, and Consequence Management

Dealing with the possibility of terrorists using these weapons of mass destruction requires some adjustment and reconsideration of the prescriptions that remain applicable to more ordinary and traditional forms of terrorism. Several differences are particularly pertinent.

DETERRENCE

It is extremely difficult to gauge the efficacy of deterrence in any setting, and assessing its importance in discouraging terrorism is even more difficult. Analytically, deterrence of anything from street crime to biological terrorism may rely on fear of consequences such as prison or execution imposed by governments or on fear of social condemnation. We can say some things about our ability to affect these aspects of deterrence.

Although the harms from a terrorist's use of weapons of mass destruction may be thousands of times as great as those of traditional terrorism, there is no way that we can greatly increase the severity of the governmentally imposed consequences for individual terrorists; these are about as great as we can make them already. Perhaps we could increase the risk of detection by offering and publicizing very large rewards for reporting, and realistic sanctions for failing to report, information relevant to anyone's development or acquisition of a weapon of mass destruction.

On the other hand, the severity of sanctions will change in the case of state-sponsored terrorism. We can assume that any nation that considered the possibility of being caught sponsoring nuclear or biological terrorism against the United States would have to anticipate massive retaliation. Only in that sense does this aspect of deterrence change with the possibility of terrorist use of weapons of mass destruction.

The other part of deterrence—the sense of widespread condemnation of the behavior—would, should, and must be very different for nuclear or biological weapons. Many relatively familiar forms of terrorism are applauded among the friends and supporters of the terrorists. The sense that this would not be true of a biological weapon may be one of the reasons we have been spared that horror. The use of biological weapons by a nation is forbidden by a treaty that almost every modern nation has signed, and the condemnation of use is not dependent on ideology or nationality.

One very important way to use the prospect of world outrage to discourage terrorism with weapons of mass destruction is to make clear how broadly the world community condemns their use. Professor Matthew Meselson of Harvard University has, for example, led in the drafting of a proposed international treaty to make it a crime *in every country* for someone to develop biological or chemical weapons *in any country*. The treaty would have intimidating effects in threatening prosecution and conviction, but it would also strengthen and broaden the barrier public rejection poses to any use of such weapons.

PREVENTION

Forms of prevention other than the ingredients of deterrence—adverse consequences and social condemnation—have always been important because of the huge political and psychological impact of terrorism. But these non-deterrent forms of prevention become vastly more important when the question is preventing use of a weapon of mass destruction. We know of three such additional methods of prevention. First, a nation can monitor groups suspected of planning terrorism in order to prevent their actions or to arrest and incapacitate them. Second, a state can seek to deny such groups what they need in the way of knowledge, materials, financial and other support, and access to carry out acts of terrorism. For example, access into the United States or to targets within the United States can be carefully controlled; financial assistance can be forbidden; and activities necessary for particular forms of terrorism, such as the purchase of equipment needed for a biological weapon, can be forbidden or regulated.

The final form of prevention is a variation of the first two: monitoring the acquisition of the various supplies or information or access that terrorists need and then using that information to detect groups more likely to be contemplating acts of terrorism so that the groups may be watched. Professor Richard Falkenrath of Harvard University's Kennedy School of Government has suggested one way to do this: develop a computer-based capacity to identify combinations of common actions, including purchases, which are unusual enough as combinations to suggest the purpose of building a weapon. Reliance on monitoring may be critical when the identity of those contemplating political violence is likely to be unknown, and especially when the outright prohibition of selling certain forms of knowledge or materials would be too burdensome on those who would use the knowledge or materials for perfectly legitimate purposes.

CONSEQUENCE MANAGEMENT

Finally, just as certain types of prevention become far more important and take on different forms when dealing with weapons of mass destruction, the same is true with regard to the other broad aim of governments facing terrorist threats. Consequence management to deal with the after-effects of terrorist use of a weapon of mass destruction would require the availability of unusual resources or resources in unusual quantities. The capacities for consequence management that are needed for ordinary forms of terrorism— relatively limited rescue and health resources and the ability to deal with psychological and political consequences by, among other things, capturing the perpetrators—are far from adequate for dealing with the after-effects of a weapon of mass destruction.

The Dilemmas of Preparation

The heart of preparation for prevention or consequence management to deal with terrorist use of a weapon of mass destruction is getting into place the committed human and physical resources, skills, and advance training, plans, and legal authority that we would want if and when a threat or actual use took place. The rational calculation is straightforward even if difficult. To list those resources and capacities we must imagine a variety of terrorist scenarios and the needs of different stages of each. To determine how much attention we would give to each different scenario and every stage of each, we have to guess at probabilities and try to develop information to enlighten the guesses. To decide what total cost and inconvenience should be borne to get all the needed capacities in place, we must use the estimates of the likelihood that they would eventually be needed and the amount by which their availability could reduce the resulting damage.

But more than an extremely difficult investment calculation is involved. Political leaders are not particularly good at encouraging present expenditures for remote and somewhat unlikely contingencies; nor are they good at insisting that constituents think about ugly matters that they would rather not think about. Not just foresight but also remarkable leadership will be required to incur expenses now for stockpiling the human skills, the organizational capacities and arrangements, and the scarce physical resources we would need in the unlikely event of a terrorist attack with nuclear or biological weapons. Also, providing the legal authority we would want on that occasion poses threats to civil liberties that no one wants to assume needlessly.

These political problems lie at the core of the issue of preparing for terrorist use of weapons of mass destruction. A large part of the answer lies in a wise use of political and psychological realities. Take first the issue of physical and human resources. The physical resources and the trained human resources are far more likely to be made available and to be maintained in operating condition if they serve dual purposes. Equipment and manpower that are also useful for a natural catastrophe would be such "dual purpose" assets. Organizational structures that are also needed in other situations— for example to coordinate the activities of different agencies and political jurisdictions in fighting forest fires—are more likely to be maintained.

Some physical resources will have to be specially acquired; some individuals, specially trained; some plans, designed for the particular event. But the ability to obtain and maintain these assets will depend significantly on whether other uses can be found for them simultaneously. Epidemics have characteristics similar to biological terrorism. Earthquakes have characteristics not unlike a vast explosion. The British have recognized this in building their own capacities. We will have to do so as well.

Second, careful planning can also help with regard to obtaining the necessary legal authority to prevent, or deal with the aftermath of, attacks by organizations planning nuclear or biological terrorism: to discover their plans and membership in advance; to monitor their activities; to interfere with their capacity to obtain crucial ingredients or knowledge; to be alerted when they have sought to obtain these assets; to assess the validity of a threat; to locate a weapon before it goes off; and to manage the consequences of use of a nuclear or biological weapon. These authorities to regulate, prohibit, search, arrest, and more—which are dangerous to the normal functioning of a democracy but may be necessary in extraordinary circumstances—must be designed for protection against misuse in ordinary times as well as for use in extraordinary times.

The task with regard to legal authority is the opposite of the task with regard to other resources. For new legal powers, we must avoid "dual purpose" authority in order to prevent the use of dangerous legal authority except in the most demanding of circumstances. We must and should devise ways to be sure that extraordinary powers are only available in extraordinary circumstances, perhaps circumstances ratified by a court at the President's personal request on the basis of a factual determination (for example, that 10,000 or more lives are at risk). We must find ways to make sure that extraordinary powers are limited in time as well as space, perhaps automatically expiring after a few weeks.

All this is the work of the future. It is obviously beginning already with vast expenditures of federal funds. Much of the task of common sense in battling the terrorist threats of the twenty-first century will remain as I have described in this volume. But some of the task is to discover sensible ways of investing and preparing now to be ready to address unlikely threats of immense harms by nuclear or biological weapons in the future.

Preface

The simple message of this book is that we can and must deal intelligently and dispassionately with a resurgent phenomenon, terrorism, that is designed to replace reason with fear and anger. It is about the use of violence for political purposes within a country—an area where crime meets politics. It is also about the use of this tactic for affecting politics by one nation against another—an area where crime meets low-level war and foreign policy. Above all, the book is a broad prescription of calm common sense, documented by more detailed applications of that prescription, as the remedy for any great democracy. Without denying that sometimes terrorist acts are the result of pure irrational rage or frustration, I focus on the more calculating forms of political violence and the responses that the United States can adopt that do not threaten its institutions.

The Case for Common Sense

For democratic nations, the primary concerns in dealing with terrorism are to maintain and protect life, the liberties necessary to a vibrant democracy, and the unity of the society, the loss of which can turn a healthy and diverse nation into a seriously divided and violent one. The message of this book is, quite simply, that preserving these three values—and not simply destroying each manifestation of terrorism as it arises—is the real goal of a democratic society, and that accomplishing this goal requires a full survey of the strange and complicated borderland where terrorism exists. What is needed most is common sense.

In this regard, my essay is a response to those like Prime Minister Benjamin Netanyahu who see the goal of those dealing with terrorism as unitary—the destruction of a deeply evil activity and of those who practice it—and who see the primary means to that destruction as simply unleashing the security forces of a powerful state. I will spell out how we can preserve life without losing liberty or unity and without setting aside law.

I work from the assumption that our stability, our security, and our capacity to meet terrorist threats effectively are all very great compared to the dangers we have faced and are likely to face. That will remain so as long as terrorism does not shift into a new dimension we have not faced: the use of weapons of mass destruction. So we can afford—we must afford—to preserve our liberties and our unity at the same time as we deal with threats to our security. For a great democratic nation, what is needed is a strategy, not unbridled anger.

The anger is hardly surprising. A recitation of the terrorist events in our recent history is a reminder of high drama and often tragedy that have seized the attention and fanned the fears of Americans in a way that little else can. In that sense, at least, terrorism is a central feature of contemporary history and contemporary awareness.

To a surprising extent, the concerns of Americans about their safety have involved the activities of the Unabomber, who sent mail bombs to those he believed were threatening the environment; the bombing of the federal building in Oklahoma City resulting in hundreds of dead and injured, apparently in protest of the federal government's actions during the standoff at the Branch Davidian complex in Waco, Texas that followed a failed attempt to seize illegal firearms and resulted in a catastrophic fire killing over 70 people; the bombing of the World Trade Center and the threatened bombing of the Holland Tunnel and other sites in New York City by militant Muslim fundamentalists protesting America's cultural and political role in the world; the assassination of Israeli Prime Minister Yitzhak Rabin by radical Jews in Israel, followed by the suicide bombings of Israeli buses by Hamas radicals, which led to a new government and a probable defeat for a cherished American foreign policy; the 1993 U.S. attack on Baghdad in retaliation for an attempt to murder former

President Bush in Kuwait; the bombing of Pan Am Flight 103 over Lockerbie, Scotland; the seizure of the *Achille Lauro* off Egypt and the killing of Leon Klinghoffer; the hijacking of TWA Flight 847 to Beirut and the murder of a navy diver; the bombing of American soldiers in a Berlin disco and the U.S. bombing of Libya in response; the shooting of American tourists in the airports of Vienna and Rome; the suicide bombings of the U.S. Marine barracks and Embassy in Beirut and the U.S. Air Force complex in Riyadh a decade later; and more. The list goes on and on without even adding the events abroad that have also jarred our consciousness: poison gas distributed by the Aum Shinrikyo sect in Japan, continual bombings by the Irish Republican Army (IRA) in England and Northern Ireland, the suicide bombings in Jerusalem in 1997, the campaign of bombs in Paris in the mid-1980s and again in the mid-1990s, etc.

The need for common sense is based on something less apparent than the amount of concern these events have generated and the vividness of the memories they leave. They are not instances of random violence. Behind them there is purpose. Terrorism is generally a calculated move in a political game. When the targets of one player, the terrorist group, are American citizens, it is generally because the terrorists intend to force the United States government into becoming the other player. The drama, the tragedy, the startling vividness of the memories—in short, the terror—are generally the calculated results of carefully selected steps intended to affect domestic or international politics. The effort may be to reduce the credibility of a government or to change particular policies or to strengthen a rival movement. In each case, the objective is political.

From the point of view of our government—of any democratic government—there are always two objectives: to save the lives of citizens and, at the same time, not to lose credibility or independence or stability. The task is harder than it seems. The government must act in a context of intense domestic political pressure to "do something"; must avoid directing anger against any sizeable segment of the population, a step that in the long run creates instability and encourages support for violent opposition; and must deal with the fears that its responses are sure to create among any people wise enough to know that government is most dangerous when it claims to be fighting dangerous enemies. Often, it must at the same time worry about its international relations with both enemies and allies. Its decisions are influenced by bureaucratic competition among law enforcement and intelligence agencies at federal and local levels, each of whom may think it knows best how to prevent further violence and how to bring the perpetrators to justice.

In such a complicated game, even a government that plays its cards perfectly may not have a winning hand. For example, when in the spring of 1996 suicide bombers from Hamas killed scores of Israeli citizens in an effort to create fear on the part of Jews—and thereby to generate a repression of Palestinian Arabs that would increase hatred on their side—the apparent objective of slowing or stopping the peace process between Israel and the PLO was attainable. Hamas had the cards and played them well. There was probably no way that Israel's Prime Minister Shimon Peres could, all at the same time, satisfy the domestic pressures so as to be able to hold office with an election pending, support Arafat's tenuous hold on Palestinian loyalties, and deal with the dangers to any peace process posed by spreading fear and anger in both populations. The election of a new prime minister, Benjamin Netanyahu, and the slowing of the peace process that resulted, reflected new currents of public opinion that had been created intentionally by acts of political violence. So did a new wave of Hamas suicide bombings in 1997.

This book is about the "political" aspect of political violence. It is about what the government of the United States can do and what we can learn from the experience of other countries, as well as our own, about how to handle both the physical and political dangers of terrorism. It is about what can be done, what actions will do more harm than good, what makes the situation difficult to handle, and how to distinguish what is extremely dangerous from what is merely dangerous. It is about common sense, about putting out fires with water rather than gasoline.

In the final analysis, the message of this book is that reason is essential to dealing with a tactic that, in most cases, only appears to be senseless. Terrorism is in fact generally calculated, and sometimes successful. Minimizing that success is very much in the interest of democracies, but to do so requires intelligence more than passion, and calculation more than anger. In this book I try to explain the political context of terrorism in the plainest of terms, with a minimum of footnotes or other references, so that a non-expert reader can understand a complicated area of passionate concern in a few hours of reading.

Advocates and Performers of Political Violence

Although this essay is about governmental responses to terrorism, not about terrorist groups, and although it is the tactics of terrorists and their intended effect on us, more than the great diversity of their motivations, that form the setting for our responses, it is important to have at least a rough sense of the types of people behind the tactics. So let me briefly introduce two of the characters who have emerged from anonymity to capture the attention of a great nation: Mahmud Abouhalima, who helped make and test the bomb that blew up at the World Trade Center on February 26, 1993, killing six people and injuring thousands; and Timothy McVeigh, convicted of the bombing of the Alfred P. Murrah Federal Building in Oklahoma City shortly after 9:00 A.M. on April 19, 1995, killing 169.

Born in Egypt, Mahmud Abouhalima grew up poor but graduated from Cairo University.[1] Eventually, he emigrated to America, using a fraudulently obtained "green card." He then went to Afghanistan to fight for the Mujahedeen forces supported by the Central Intelligence Agency (CIA). Injured, he returned to the United States with many other Islamic militants and continued his work at a center designed to coordinate volunteers to fight in the Afghan war. The volunteers called it "The Service for Jihad Office."

What brought Abouhalima together with a sizeable number of others in mosques and other centers in New Jersey and New York was a shared set of beliefs with a long history. They believed passionately that religious duty required taking radical action to bring the institutions of society more in line with the commands of their scripture.

As such, they were on the radical fringe of Islamic beliefs. Virtually all believing Muslims consider their scripture (the Qur' n) the literal word of God; they thus qualify as "fundamentalists" according to the most common idea of fundamentalism among Americans. Indeed, most Muslims consider the Qur' n to be not only God's word but also in main part God's commands, which all Muslims are obligated to obey.

Within the Muslim religion, a large subset of adherents support action to implement religion and religious law as the blueprint for life and society here and now. In other words, these "fundamentalists" oppose secularism as practiced in the West. A smaller subset of these believe in using politics toward that end. These we might describe as adherents to "political Islam" or as "Islamists." Finally, a radical fringe of this smallest group believe in using violence to the same end. Abouhalima and his associates would place themselves among this radical fringe as supporters of "Islamic" political violence.

To those like Abouhalima, Sheik Omar Abdel-Rahman was a spiritual leader in the wars against secular and corrupt governments in the Arab states, the Soviet Union in Afghanistan, and Israel, as well as against the United States, the leader of what they perceive to be the corrupt and godless forces of the West. Sheik Abdel-Rahman had also been born in Egypt, where he became blind at the age of ten. He pursued a deeply religious education, studying at Al-Azar University, the Islamic world's most prestigious institution of higher learning and the oldest university in the world. There he adopted the violent strands of Islamic thought, which originated in the fourteenth century as a defense against the inroads of the Mongols.

Soon after graduating from Al-Azar, Sheik Omar Abdel-Rahman began preaching in earnest against the secular governments of Abdul Gamal al-Nasser and Anwar Sadat, ending up in prison on several occasions. In his 1985 autobiography, he explains his opposition to successive Egyptian governments:

The state allows adultery and creates the opportunity for it, the state organized night clubs and prepared special police to protect adulterers and prostitutes. Liquor factories are built by the state. Doesn't this deny God's laws?[2]

During the 1980s, the Egyptian state became more and more repressive of Islamists, many of whom were, like the Sheik, providing the ideological underpinnings of a terrorist campaign. Tapes of the Sheik's talks were circulating throughout the poor neighborhoods of Egypt urging followers to, for example, "hit hard and kill the enemies of God in every spot to rid [the state] of the descendants of apes and pigs fed at the tables of Zionism, Communism, and Imperialism."[3]

The Sheik was also coming to play a religious role in sanctioning specific violent acts by fundamentalists. In the traditional Islamic legal system, laws derive from the Qur'n, understood as the word of God as revealed by the Angel Gabriel to the Prophet Mohammed in seventh-century Arabia. Since the Qur'n is often cryptic and does not offer a complete system of rules for society, it must be supplemented. The Hadith, second-hand stories of the Prophet, illustrate various moral precepts, or *sunna*, that Mohammed established by word or example. Since even orthodox Islam recognizes the danger that some Hadith are apocryphal, a scholar is needed to weigh the authenticity of the Hadith and to apply both sources of Islamic law to any situation. When serving as an authority on religions, this scholar, known as *atim* or *mufti*, will issue a legal and moral opinion (there is no distinction in traditional Islamic law) to guide believers. This opinion is known as a *fatwa*. However, since a secular state does not grant a mufti's opinions any legally binding force, a *fatwa*'s authority is unclear. If, on due reflection, a believer accepts a particular scholar as a pious and fully qualified interpreter of the law, then he may follow the *fatwas* of that scholar with a clear conscience.

Sheik Omar Abdel-Rahman's opinions derived from his particularly radical interpretation of Islam, and were often interpreted by his followers as *fatwas* justifying particular actions. In 1980, Sheik Abdel-Rahman was tried twice for allegedly issuing a *fatwa* that justified the assassination of Anwar Sadat; in both cases, he was acquitted. Later in the 1980s, Sheik Abdel-Rahman was accused of issuing a *fatwa* that justified the killing of Christians in Fayoum, where he preached. Again, he was acquitted. In both cases, Sheik Abdel-Rahman defended his actions as an exercise of his own freedom of thought and religion, denying that his religious opinions ever advocated specific acts of violence. His lawyer argued that the Jihad Organization, which assassinated Sadat, "asked for a religious stand about a ruler who is ruling against Islamic law. [Sheik Abdel-Rahman] did not specify Sadat and the members of the Jihad Organization did not specify Sadat for him."[4] Yet, regardless of the specificity of his advice, his followers thought it was clear. His trial became a platform for his religious and political criticisms of the Egyptian government. "Our duty to God is more binding than our duty to the President of the Republic. We owe God obedience and no obedience is owed to him who disobeys God," he declared.[5] He was acquitted.

Near the end of the 1980s, Sheik Abdel-Rahman became involved in the religious war against the Soviet regime in Afghanistan. He inspired thousands of volunteers from the Arab world—financed by the U.S. Central Intelligence Agency—to fight with the Mujahedeen against the atheist invaders and to create a true Islamic republic in an independent Afghanistan. The CIA distributed over $3 billion to arm the Afghan rebels, including vehemently anti-American factions.

After the sheik returned to Egypt, he found it necessary to escape to Sudan, and from there fled to the United States, taking advantage of a mistake by U.S. immigration authorities supposed to be checking a terrorist "watch" list. In the United States, he soon became the spiritual leader of a politically violent fringe of Islamists who had gathered there and organized around support for the war in Afghanistan. Abouhalima, who had first become attracted to the sheik's ideas in Egypt, became his driver and one of his followers. He later took part in the murder of the radical Jewish extremist Rabbi Meir Kahane.

On September 1, 1992, the technical mastermind for the first major Islamic terrorist campaign in the United States arrived at New York's John F. Kennedy Airport: Ramzi Yousef, a highly trained, sophisticated, and well-financed terrorist from Pakistan and the Afghan jihad. He slipped through immigration by presenting a valid Iraqi passport and applied for asylum, swearing he would face persecution by Iraqi guards if he returned to Iraq. The Immigration and Naturalization Service, unable to interview him on the spot, paroled him into the country over the advice of a line official. Abouhalima promptly helped Yousef get a professional driver's license for identification. Within six months, they had completed their preparations and, on February 26, 1993, they mounted the explosion that ripped through level B-2 of the underground parking garage of the World Trade Center. Yousef escaped to Pakistan that evening and, as I will later discuss, continued to plot and execute terrorist acts around the globe. Abouhalima, after a federal trial in New York, is now serving out a 240-year prison sentence for his role in the bombing.

Timothy McVeigh, the central player in the Oklahoma City bombing, was born in Pendleton, New York in 1968.[6] McVeigh and one of his two sisters were left with his father when his parents were divorced and his mother moved to Florida. He was quiet, average, and unmemorable during his high school years. He briefly became a survivalist, stockpiling food and weapons. Both the preparations for an apocalyptic future and the love of collecting and using weapons remained with him.

He was unable to find a good job after graduating from high school and complained that he was going nowhere. Some of his behavior during this period seems bizarre. A co-worker in a security firm said McVeigh gave him a ride home driving at 70 miles per hour, yelling at slower drivers, and grabbing at a shotgun "like he was going to blow them away." The co-worker said that "sometimes when I was driving, he'd put his face right next to mine and scream that the cars were going too slow, and then just keep his face there and stare at me."[7]

At the suggestion of friends, McVeigh enlisted in the Army, where his love of guns and explosives combined with a sense of belonging. He showed some real promise as a soldier, fought in Iraq, and then applied for the Green Berets. His failure to make that elite group seems to have been a personal disaster. He took an early discharge, then drifted from job to job and state to state. He lost weight and appeared unstable.

During this period in his early twenties, acquaintances described him as having a growing obsessive belief that the federal government was conspiring to enslave the American people, and that it would have to be stopped, at any cost, by the few patriots with clear vision. By early 1992, Timothy McVeigh was writing letters to newspapers, complaining of crime, taxes, and political corruption, and warning:

Do we have to shed blood to reform the current system? I hope it doesn't come to that, but it might.[8]

McVeigh's anger and distrust for the government were nourished by two events. First was the standoff between separatist Randy Weaver and federal law enforcement officials at Ruby Ridge, Idaho in August, 1992. Weaver, wanted on firearms charges, was unwilling to appear for trial. The U.S. Marshal Service tried to capture him. After Weaver's son Samuel and a federal marshal were killed in a gunfight, an FBI sniper, Lon Horiuchi, accidentally shot and killed Weaver's wife, Vicki, while she held her ten-month-old daughter inside the cabin. Many criticized the federal government's decision to relax its shooting rules during the standoff, blaming overly zealous law enforcement for the death of Weaver's wife.

Less than a year later, McVeigh's suspicion of the federal government was sealed by the federal raid on the compound of the Branch Davidian religious sect in Waco, Texas. Officials from the Bureau of Alcohol, Tobacco and Firearms (ATF) were prevented by armed force from arresting David Koresh and others. After a 51-day standoff, federal officials stormed the Branch Davidian compound. The ensuing fire, apparently set by the Davidians, took the lives of over 70 people. To McVeigh, Waco was simply another example of the government's willingness to trample the rights of American citizens. In symbolic retaliation, McVeigh bombed the federal building in Oklahoma City on the anniversary of the Waco disaster.

Like those involved in the bombing of the World Trade Center, McVeigh's willingness and capacity to act was inspired by others holding similar beliefs. While McVeigh did not formally belong to any organized group as Abouhalima did, he read the same literature, watched the same motion pictures, subscribed to the same magazines, and at least occasionally attended the same meetings as the members of various right-wing militias across America.[9] *Time* magazine wrote of McVeigh's attachment to Andrew Macdonald's *The Turner Diaries*, which was published in 1978 and tells the story of a group of white supremacists who blow up FBI headquarters in Washington.[10] The book is heavily racist and anti-Semitic. McVeigh was so devoted to the book that he handed it out to friends and sold it at gun shows, even at a loss. A photocopy of a passage from the *Turner Diaries* explaining that the purpose of the fictional bombing was "to wake up America" was in McVeigh's car when he was arrested shortly after the Oklahoma City bombing.

The militias appear relevant to the Oklahoma City bombing mainly for indicating how many Americans there are with views like McVeigh's. The total membership of the various militias across the United States is estimated by the Southern Poverty Law Center to be between ten and fifteen million. As many as a hundred thousand may be quite active members. United by an extreme libertarian philosophy and a deep suspicion of government and the establishment press, the movement has roots in all regions of the country. Its concerns are not only the right to bear arms but also the enjoyment of property rights free of any governmental regulation, freedom of movement without the licensing requirements that accompany automobile use, a right to deny the use of taxes to fund programs that they consider unethical or immoral, a concern about the place of religion in American life, and an acute sense of the loss of allegiance to what is distinctly "American" as a definable set of views and experiences.

Obviously, most of the subscribers to these views are not violent, but many do believe that the government and the press have become tools of an enemy agenda. Trusting in books like Gary Allen's *None Dare Call It Conspiracy* and Pat Robertson's *The New World Order*, people within the militias fear a conspiratorial organization of "One Worlders" who are using their considerable influence to create an environment where a world government can take control of the United States. For some of these, the "one world" government is identified with the Antichrist, whom they expect will stand in opposition to Christ in the last days before the Second Coming. The identification creates a mixture of patriotism and Christianity in support of their program.

Concluding that the government has abdicated its role as guarantor of the liberties outlined in the Constitution's Bill of Rights, many members of the militia believe that it is time to arm themselves in defense of their liberties. They reason that the Declaration of Independence itself says that "whenever any form of government becomes destructive of these ends [life, liberty, and the pursuit of happiness], it is the Right of the People to alter or abolish it." They believe that their liberties are being steadily eroded by a corrupt and deceptive government and press that may be trying to usher in the age of the Antichrist in the form of United Nations control of our country. Therefore, they argue, it may be time to heed Thomas Jefferson's advice that the tree of liberty must be watered periodically with the blood of patriots and tyrants. This advice was printed on Timothy McVeigh's favorite t-shirt.

Both the similarities between McVeigh and Abouhalima and the differences between them are worth noting.

Both bombers were part of wider social networks that supported their fundamental beliefs, even if not their willingness to carry them into violent action. They were the radical fringe of groups that were themselves outside the political spectrum that feels it has influence and respect in the United States. (In Europe, the broader groups would thus be called "extra-parliamentary.") Their actions were addressed to this supportive audience as well as to the American people at large.

The perpetrators shared the same knowledge of technology and access to needed ingredients of bombs. Both had even received military training by the United States. The two groups of bombers had ready access to a target that would carry their message to the American people—in one case, the World Trade Center as a symbol of materialism, in the other, the Oklahoma City federal building as a symbol of governmental overreaching that threatened individual freedoms.

For acts of massive violence, conscience needs a solvent. Both McVeigh and Abouhalima lived in an atmosphere of frenzied speech, where a violent response to government was urged or justified by leaders within the broader group. Each had elaborate and persuasive explanations of why the normal rules of civilized behavior did not apply to him.

In most of these characteristics, the bombers of the World Trade Center and the bombers of the federal building in Oklahoma City also resemble the terrorists of the left and the nationalist terrorists who have operated in Italy, Germany, France, Northern Ireland, and Israel. For example, the profile fits, almost perfectly, the group involved in the successful plot to assassinate Prime Minister Yitzhak Rabin of Israel in 1995.

From the point of view of counter-terrorist policy, however, there are also extremely important differences. Abouhalima was a member of a fairly well-structured group, closely related to supporters abroad that might even include foreign governments. The movement of which Abouhalima's group was a part had a history. The foreign connections and the continuity made the group more dangerous. Because of its roots and branches abroad, rounding up the suspects would require rare international cooperation of the sort that eventually led to the arrest of Yousef in Pakistan. (See Chapter 4.)

But the size and history of the group also created vulnerabilities. The United States could have prevented several leading conspirators from coming into the country: their records were well known. A number of them even appear to have been involved in other forms of violence in the United States—particularly, the assassination of Rabbi Meir Kahane. Aware of such violent activities, the FBI placed an informant within the group. Perhaps the explosion could have been prevented. In any event, once it had occurred the chances of identifying likely suspects were great, and this is the hardest step in a terrorist investigation.

When one considers prevention or prosecution, the Oklahoma City bombing looks very different indeed. McVeigh's personal history made him a candidate for some form of explosive violence. He gravitated to the intellectual world of the militias, pulling with him two army friends. The federal assaults at Waco and Ruby Ridge on loners who believed, like McVeigh, that guns were a necessary protection against government helped unhinge him. But there is nothing in his background or in these events that would have suggested that his activities should have been monitored for terrorist activity. In this he differed significantly from the bombers of the World Trade Center. In many ways, McVeigh may be closer to loners like Roland Smith, Jr., a New York man who in December 1995 responded to an atmosphere of racial hatred by setting fire to a Harlem clothing store and gunning down those attempting to flee; or John Salvi, who in 1994 emerged from the fringes of the anti-abortion movement to kill a receptionist at each of two abortion clinics in Brookline, Massachusetts. One might even compare McVeigh to Theodore Kaczynski, convicted in 1998 as the Unabomber who sent letter bombs to a number of people he believed were destroying the environment.

There is no organization that can be infiltrated to prevent such acts. Although the perpetrators may not be protected by the assistance or silence of a sympathetic segment of the population, they are also far less likely to be known than other terrorists. Indeed, a highly intelligent bomber working alone and pursuing an unknown cause, or a cause shared by too many for all to be treated as suspects, can carry on a course of political violence for years, as Theodore Kaczynski demonstrated.

What Lies Ahead

Chapter 1 examines the differences in definitions of terrorism and the difficulties of placing it within more familiar contexts of crime, warfare, or politics. It introduces the extraordinary impact on democratic politics that terrorism can have and examines the consequences of that impact. It explores the mechanisms through which terrorism may work to affect democratic politics, focusing on the audiences to which it may be addressed.

The chapters that follow are broadly organized around a central distinction between international and domestic terrorism. The problems are different and so are the powers of the government in dealing with them. Moreover, the prevalence of international terrorism contrasts dramatically with the rarity of domestic terrorism.

In this last respect, the dramatic and frightening attacks by terrorists on the World Trade Center and the Oklahoma City federal building are, fortunately, relatively rare cases of terrorism within the United States. In 1994, there were no domestic terrorist incidents on U.S. soil, while there were 66 attacks on U.S. citizens abroad. So, international terrorism is not only a different problem from domestic terrorism and not only a problem that must be addressed with different powers. It is also a problem the prevalence of which suggests special attention.

The line between international and domestic terrorism is not generally drawn on the basis of the location of an attack but rather on the basis of the involvement of more than one country. The U.S. Department of State has long defined international terrorism as "terrorism involving citizens or the territory of more than one country." That includes the situation in which Americans are most subject to terrorism: attacks on Americans or U.S. diplomatic missions or American-owned property abroad. But it would also include an attack within the United States by citizens of another country or by terrorists using the assistance or territory of another country, such as the World Trade Center bombing.

The United States has generally been the leading target of international terrorism taking place outside our borders because it is the world's greatest power and its foreign policy is influential throughout the world. Inevitably, this influence is contrary to the interests of various groups that are prepared to use violence. American targets are particularly attractive when they are outside our borders. The attack creates an international sensation. Moreover, the location can be chosen in a place where U.S. intelligence and prevention are least effective and, perhaps most important of all, where the chance of arrest and punishment are minimized.

Because of the importance and relative prevalence of international terrorism, the four chapters that follow the introduction focus on this issue, beginning with the role of intelligence in Chapter 2, then turning in Chapter 3 to the choices presented when a hostage situation or an ongoing terrorist campaign must be addressed. Chapter 4 examines the possibilities of international cooperation as a remedy, and Chapter 5 looks at military retaliation and its prospects when terrorism is supported by another state.

The risks and the possibilities are very different when the terrorism takes place at home. Far more significant efforts at prevention can be undertaken. Law enforcement can operate without the cooperation of foreign governments, although terrorism places unusual strains on a criminal justice system. Intelligence gathering is subject to more careful rules at home than abroad, but many more sources are likely to be available. Chapters 6, 7, and 8 turn to these issues of domestic terrorism.

Chapter 6 explores the logic of preventive steps to make terrorist activities more difficult or riskier. Chapter 7 turns to investigation and prosecution of terrorism when prevention has failed. Chapter 8 examines the critical role of intelligence gathering and processing—and the special dangers of this activity—in a context of U.S. citizens contemplating violent politics. The concluding chapter, Chapter 9, summarizes what common sense can tell us about dealing with politically motivated violence.

Terrorism and America

Chapter 1

An Introduction to Terrorism

The Federal Bureau of Investigation reports that in the decade after 1985 there were only two terrorist incidents on U.S. soil with substantial foreign involvement (i.e., "international terrorism"): the bombing of the World Trade Center in February 1993, and an all-but-ignored occupation of the Iranian Mission to the United Nations by five opponents of the regime in 1992. During the first half of the 1990s we had 32 domestic incidents of terrorism, of which 9 occurred in a single night in 1993 when small incendiary devices were placed in department stores by one of the most active domestic terrorist groups, animal rights activists. The number of attacks on U.S. individuals abroad has fallen to less than a third of what it was in 1986, with 66 attacks in 1994, a year in which there were no domestic terrorists incidents in the United States.

Why then the immense attention to terrorism in the later 1990s in the United States? It is true that U.S. citizens have been among the leading victims of international terrorist events, including the downing of Pan Am Flight 103 in 1988 over Lockerbie, Scotland; the 1985 hijacking of the *Achille Lauro*; the machine gunnings in the same year of the airports of Rome and Vienna; and the 1983 suicide bombings of U.S. marine headquarters in Beirut. Still, home felt safe. That feeling of security at home was shattered by the bombings of the World Trade Center in 1993 with nearly 1000 injured and of the Oklahoma City federal building in 1995 with 169 killed. These events, terrible enough in themselves, raised the possibility of a sustained campaign of violence on U.S. soil. This side of the Atlantic suddenly seemed to be exposed to political violence of the sort that the United States had escaped while other democracies had not. Germany, Italy, and Spain, for example, lived through sustained terrorist campaigns in the 1970s and 1980s; France, Great Britain, and Israel had suffered the same in the 1990s as well.

Added to this was a fear that a terrorist repertoire that had been limited to assassination, conventional bombing, hostage-taking, and hijacking might be dangerously expanded. American apprehensions, reflected in dramatic Congressional hearings, grew with the use of poison gas in Tokyo subways by the Aum Shinrikyo cult in Japan. The possibility that the use of nuclear, biological, or chemical weapons might be added to the terrorist arsenal is chilling. At the end of 1995, John Deutch, then the new director of the CIA, described terrorism as one of the major threats facing the United States.[1]

Such events, the fears they excite, and the reactions they invite are the subject of this book. It is about violent activity designed to create grave public apprehension in order to convey, with awesome force, the terrorists' message. And it is about governmental responses. Deep and broad national fears of terrorism create grave political problems for a government. Immense popular concern makes acts of terrorism exceptionally tempting occasions for political opponents of the administration in power to make the evil appear far clearer and the danger far greater than they are. The Iranian taking of 52 U.S. citizens as hostages in 1979 and the futility of efforts to free them may have cost U.S. President Jimmy Carter an election. In the context of a terrorist act or campaign, the political risks to an administration of inaction or even caution are very grave. But wise policy may counsel restraint. In terms of national well-being, the gravest national dangers from a terrorist act (short of an immense escalation of terrorist tactics) are that the interplay of terrorism, public reaction, and governmental response may sharply separate one significant group from the rest of the society or severely undermine the nation's democratic traditions.

Violence as politics has been a subject of great concern in many other democracies for generations. Although the word "terrorism" dates only from the time of the French Revolution, the acts it embraces go back to biblical times. Nor is political violence new to the United States. We have lost four presidents and two senators to assassination. We have also had our share of famous bombings, including the Haymarket Square bombing in 1886; the *Los Angeles Times* bombing in 1910; the San Francisco Preparedness Day bombing in 1916; and the Wall Street bombing in 1920. And we have had groups such as the Ku Klux Klan dedicated for decades to terrorizing an important segment of our population—black Americans.

The Efforts to Define Terrorism

Only relatively recently have there been attempts to define "terrorism" as clearly as we define murder, robbery, or rape. The effort has been less than successful. Germany's internal security agency, the Office for the Protection of the Constitution, says terrorism is the "enduringly conducted struggle for political goals, which are intended to be achieved by means of assaults on the life and property of other persons, especially by means of severe crimes [such as murder, kidnapping, arson]."[2] The British "Prevention of Terrorism Act" of 1974 described terrorism as "the use of violence for political ends, and includes any use of violence for the purpose of putting the public or any section of the public in fear." The U.S. State Department treats as terrorism any violence perpetrated for political reasons by subnational groups or secret state agents, often directed at noncombatant targets, and usually intended to influence an audience. Our federal statutes (18 U.S.C. 3077) define an "act of terrorism" as any activity that involves criminal violence that "appears to be intended (i) to intimidate or coerce a civilian population; (ii) to influence the policy of a government by intimidation or coercion; or (iii) to affect the conduct of a government by assassination or kidnapping." The group of European Interior Ministers working together to deal with terrorism made a point of excluding traditional warfare: "Terrorism is . . . the use, or the threatened use, by a cohesive group of persons of violence (short of warfare) to affect political aims."

There is an appealing neutrality about state definitions of terrorism. That may not be surprising. States use violence themselves for political purposes—in wartime even against civilian populations.

The state definitions suggest that terrorists are a hostile force pursuing political ends. But other definitions, often by academics, have far more of a moral or criminal flavor.

An extremely comprehensive review of possible definitions was conducted by Professor Alex P. Schmid of Leiden University in the Netherlands. After consulting 50 scholars, he came up with a definition far too lengthy to be useful but then found a far shorter definition that was almost as accurate and more useful. Noting that there is a strong degree of consensus about what actions count as war crimes—including attacks on persons taking no active part in hostilities and also hostage-taking—and that just such attacks on the undefended are "not an unsought side-effect but a deliberate strategy" of terrorists, Schmid proposes defining acts of terrorism as "peacetime equivalents of war crimes:" acts that would, if carried out by a government in war, violate the Geneva Conventions."[3]

The various definitions differ in two ways. First, "political" and "moral" definitions differ immensely in the amount of hatred they seek to arouse. Benjamin Netanyahu, prime minister of Israel, leader of its Likud party, and author of a 1995 book, *Fighting Terrorism*, emphasizes that "terrorism is the deliberate and systematic assault on civilians to inspire fear for political ends." As such, he argues, "*nothing* justifies terrorism . . . it is evil *per se*." To his mind, "terrorism attacks the very foundations of civilization and threatens to erase it altogether by killing man's sense of sin. . . . The unequivocal and unrelenting moral condemnation of terrorism must therefore constitute the first line of defense against its most insidious effect."[4] The cold and analytic definitions of the Western governments can not convey such fury.

Second, the variety of definitions reflects very different practical and administrative reasons for defining terrorism. Consider the variety of reasons. The term is the basis of U.S. statutes that allocate money and authority for dealing with certain problems. A finding of "terrorism" determines that the U.S. government (specifically, the Federal Bureau of Investigation and the Department of Justice) will take the lead in investigating and prosecuting certain crimes that might otherwise fall within the primary jurisdiction of state or local governments. If it is "terrorism," the intelligence agencies may be involved because the crime is also a matter of national security. In international settings, the need to define terrorism may arise because some crimes, such as assaulting or killing an American abroad, are only subject to U.S. prosecution if they occur for terrorist purposes. Western allies meet to discuss what is defined, for their purposes, as terrorism, and they grant and deny cooperation in intelligence and extradition on the basis of such definitions.

Two things are clear from this list of occasions where a definition of terrorism is needed. First, we cannot escape the task of defining terrorism for each of these purposes unless we are prepared to treat politically motivated and directed violence as no different from other crimes—a decision that would be risky business and strongly contrary to public reactions in almost every country. Second, the definitions are likely to differ, not only because of different judgments about the centrality of the moral issue, but also because definitions are meant to serve the particular purposes most relevant in the setting where they are being used.

Secret state violence against its own citizens is unlikely to be treated as state terrorism in meetings of allies. This is not because there is any great moral difference from secret state terrorism directed against citizens of another government, but because such violent repression of individuals in the home country is generally a far lesser concern to the governments of countries unaffected and unlikely to be affected by the practice. So in this setting, secret state violence against its own citizens is unlikely to be called "terrorism." Violence against civilians, particularly government officials, in the context of guerrilla warfare or during a war between states is not considered terrorism in many contexts simply because it is not subject to the same remedies (which are designed for times of peace). Many modern states have resorted to aerial bombing of civilian targets in order to induce fear in wartime. For similar reasons of practicality, violence that is carried out as a mere expression of anger without expectation of changing the conduct of any group or government, might or might not be included within the responsibilities of the agency that deals with "terrorist" crimes, depending on whether it posed a continuing danger and on whether it raised the same unusual public fears as more calculated political violence.

The definitions of terrorism thus differ markedly in what they include. In this book, I focus on the core of the problem by looking only at conduct that satisfies almost all the definitions. The violence I discuss involves in most instances politically motivated activity by groups, not individuals. It is more than a nonpolitical expression of rage, and it is meant to work by raising concerns and fears, and not just by the isolated assassination of a government leader such as Israeli Prime Minister Yitzhak Rabin or U.S. President John F. Kennedy. Borrowing from our State Department's definition, it is violence conducted as part of a political strategy by a subnational group or secret agents of a foreign state (although secret and violent repression of political opponents by an authoritarian government is just as bad).

The political violence I emphasize is plainly directed at noncombatant targets; I set aside the hard question of where to place off-duty soldiers or the industrial managers producing weapons of war. The violence is directed at people, not just property, and carried out for a political purpose, although that purpose may only be partially formed. Like the Committee of Interior Ministers of the European Union, I would exclude situations of warfare. And, to preserve moral fervor, I limit "terrorism" to political violence in or against true democracies.

Every state would consider activities fitting this core definition to be "terrorism." It overlaps very substantially with Alex Schmid's definition of terrorism as behavior that would amount to war crimes if it occurred during war. Like Netanyahu, I can think of very little excuse for an assault on civilians to advance political purposes. But an excessive moralism is likely to get in the way of clear thought about what the United States should do. I favor a more sophisticated strategy than Netanyahu's recommendation that we unleash "security services to take the vigorous action needed to uproot the terror in the midst of [our society]," and use our "operational capacity to eviscerate domestic terror."[5]

Not only Netanyahu's prescription, but also his moral judgements are simpler than many would adopt. Terrorism is inexcusable in a democracy, but would it have been "evil *per se*" for a German resistance group to adopt the same targets as Allied air forces chose in Hitler's Germany? The African National Congress, Provisional Irish Republican Army, and the radical organizations of the Jewish settlers before the creation of Israel all engaged in attacks on civilian targets, and yet their leaders have been treated as heroes.

The Difficulties of Categorizing Terrorism Sensibly

The fundamental difficulties of defining terrorism are compounded by the difficulties of shaping policy for a type of behavior that fits poorly into more familiar categories. Terrorist acts are both crimes and forms of warfare, and in both respects are unlike what we are used to. Terrorism involves unique psychological phenomena—no less real for being poorly understood—used as part of a totally unfamiliar type of political strategy based on violence. The likelihood and strength of a terrorist campaign depends upon sociological factors we are not accustomed to examining; the danger to the society in which the terrorism takes place depends upon the divisions within it before the terrorism occurs. Consider each of characteristics in turn.

As a crime, terrorism is different. Most crimes are the product of greed, anger, jealousy, or the desire for domination, respect, or position in a group, and not of any desire to "improve" the state of the world or of a particular nation. Most crimes do not involve—as part of the plan for accomplishing their objectives—trying to change the occupants of government positions, their actions, or the basic structures and ideology of a nation. Some would argue that violence carried out for political purposes is more altruistic; others would vigorously deny that. But all would agree that political violence is different from ordinary crime, in that it is planned to force changes in government actions, people, structure, or even ideology as a means to whatever ends the perpetrators are seeking with whatever motivations drive them towards those ends. It is in that sense that the U.S. State Department definition says that the violence is usually "perpetrated for political reasons."

As a form of combat, terrorism falls into the category of violent ways of pursuing political ends, a category that includes war between states, civil war, guerrilla warfare, and coup d'état. It differs from these other forms of violent combat for political ends in that it is carried out during peacetime in secret, without occupying or claiming to occupy any significant territory, and without organizing large groups to defy government authority openly. Indeed, for many, the same violent acts have a different status when they accompany a civil or guerilla war. Nor are they considered "terrorism" when they accompany a war between nation states, for then they become a part of the normal craft of spies or bomber pilots rather than a form of politics or secret warfare that works primarily or exclusively through its own terrifying means.

Terrorism has traditionally used relatively unsophisticated weapons in a limited number of ways to inflict relatively little damage. Within these constraints terrorism can only hope to produce limited political results, since in almost every country the government controls vastly superior military and civilian security forces. Even such limited actions may occasionally force a change in particular occupants of office by carefully planned assassinations like those of Anwar Sadat and Yitzhak Rabin. They may even bring about a change in a particular policy by simply imposing sufficient costs upon a government that the government will choose to abandon a weakly held policy, as when the United States left Lebanon after the truck bombing of the U.S. Marine barracks in Beirut. But any broader objectives, such as pulling out of places of considerable strategic or political importance or abandoning important alliances or polices, are far more difficult and far less likely. And changing the government itself would require the politically violent group either to overpower the government's military force or to shift the loyalties of the government security forces or the public at large sufficiently that they would broadly deny their support to the state. Overthrow of a government may be the result of a civil war or a coup d'état, but it is a highly unlikely result of the relatively small-scale violence by those outside of government that we associate with terrorism.

Combining crime and armed combat, terrorism is an illegal form of clandestine warfare that is carried out by a sub-state group to change the policies, personnel, structure, or ideology of a government, or to influence the actions of another part of the population—one with enough self-identity to respond to selective violence. (The burning of African-American churches in the American South in 1996 would fall in the latter category.) Throwing domestic politics into this witches' brew, terrorism is also a form of violent domestic politics (directed at democratic regimes, if we are to retain for our definition of "terrorism" some moral clarity) carried out without organizing mass opposition.

The Politics of Violence

From the terrorists' perspective, the major force of terrorism comes not from its physical impact but from its psychological impact. Terrorism is rarely an effective form of insurgent violence in the sense of achieving its sponsors' ultimate goals, but it can cause enormous problems for democratic governments because of its impact on the psychology of great masses of citizens, the "audience" referred to in the U.S. State Department's definition. Terrorist bombings, assassinations, and hostage-taking have, in nations with a free press, the ability to hold the attention of vast populations. By generating a combination of fear and fascination, terrorists have been able to capture important parts of the agendas of great nations.

Realistic policymakers take this power of terrorism over the imagination of vast parts of the public, and the reaction to that power first by a free press and then by responsive elected officials, to be central facts of political life, whether or not the fascination and anxiety produced by terrorism can be adequately explained. The unusual power to generate mass concerns by relatively easily accomplished bombings, killings, or hostage-taking is useful to terrorists because it allows them to send extremely forceful messages to audiences who would otherwise be unaware even of their existence. That is the unusual politics of terrorism. To whom is the message sent and for what purpose? Despite what I have so far suggested, the answer is not always "the government."

The goals of terrorist groups are unrealistic in terms of the ordinary, mainstream politics of the country. To change this, terrorists sometimes address their frightening message to the center of a democratic political spectrum, to those who have been indifferent to the cause that is bringing forth violence. Part of the center's support of government policy flows from an assumption that the government can maintain order and security, and that it reaches fair results through an orderly process of decision. Terrorism can undermine this assumption. A sustained course of acts of political violence can show that safety does not necessarily flow from support of government policies.

The costs imposed by even small-scale political violence may cause people relatively indifferent to the merits of the cause to urge the government to pursue a policy of accommodation with the insurgent group in order to eliminate those costs. This objective seems to explain the long history of terrorism in Northern Ireland and Israel, which in both cases has had some measure of political success. Both the Provisional IRA and the Palestine Liberation Organization have achieved a legitimacy and encountered a spirit of accommodation that might not have been present without their campaigns.

Alternatively, the political violence may be addressed more directly to the government and its supporting elites. A campaign of assassinations may aim to cause resignations by bringing fear to those in particularly crucial positions, such as judges or prosecutors. The Italian mafia's killing in 1992 of the great anti-mafia magistrates Giovanni Falcone and Paolo Boisellino had this purpose. Threats to kill mayoral candidates by guerrilla forces opposing the government in Colombia in 1997 had this intended effect. Terrorism may simply demand so much of the attention of government leaders that they find it necessary to compromise so that they can direct their energies elsewhere. For terrorists of the law-and-order Right, acts of random violence, disguised as acts perpetrated by insurgent radicals, can be "addressed" to the attention of security forces in the hope of provoking a coup and a military takeover. Such an effort occurred in Italy in the 1970s, most dramatically with bombings of crowded facilities.

A third potential audience for terrorist acts consists of those who are potential supporters of an insurgency. Acts of terrorism can show these people that the government is not as powerful as it portrays itself, but rather is weak and vulnerable. Or terrorist acts may generate a response by the government that is repressive enough to make allies of those who would otherwise be neutral. When the terrorist cause is to create a separate state, a particularly important subcategory within the audience of potential supporters consists of foreign governments that may be brought, by public accounts of repression, to support their separatist brothers. An act of terrorism—the assassination by a Serbian nationalist of Austrian Archduke Francis Ferdinand in 1914—was a major factor in precipitating World War I because it led Austria and Germany to declare war on Serbia and Russia.

Acts of small-scale political violence can deepen social divisions within a society by increasing anger, fear, and suspicion between groups, thereby furthering the cause of an insurgent group that wants to broaden demands for a separate state for its members. And once the society is severely divided along racial, religious, or ethnic lines, acts of terrorism may allow one group to claim leadership where there are many contestants for this post. After all, violent actions can show power and ruthlessness, two attributes generally sought in leaders in difficult times. This too was a part of the terrorist strategies in Northern Ireland and Israel.

A final audience of terrorist violence may be the active members of the terrorist group itself. Setting aside the ordinary crimes that may be committed to finance the violent organization, terrorist group members may engage in violence because dramatic actions are necessary to maintain the group's morale and self-esteem. In addition, the threat of punishment at the hands of the government for playing a role in violent acts of terrorism may lock in members who might otherwise quit. Violence is also frequently the means of punishing informers and even those who have merely left the group, and the means of sending a message to others who might contemplate the same actions.

However, it may be a mistake to classify audiences and messages too finely. Many acts of political violence are relatively uncalculated, and represent a desperate effort to be heard, i.e., to push a handful of people or their concerns onto the national stage, where attention is generally monopolized by presidents and senators, governors and mayors, cabinet officers and media stars. For many people there is no other way to get onto the stage of national attention for their policies, resentments, or personality. Most of us agree not to be on that stage and to be satisfied with the role of voters or contributors or persuaders. But a determination to be a far more central player can lead individuals to take the only readily available shortcut to world-wide prominence, and that may be to link a violent act to a deeply felt cause.

The Effectiveness of Terrorism

How can limited violence to convey a message hope to affect the policies of a modern democratic state? Often, it cannot. The terrorists are simply mistaken about their prospects or, perhaps like Timothy McVeigh, so angry that they are indifferent to them. But in two situations, terrorism can and does affect the policies of modern democratic states. First, it can be effective when it is operating in a country whose population is already severely divided into suspicious and hostile groups. That has been the situation, for example, in Northern Ireland, Israel, India, Sri Lanka, Spain, and a number of other states. Second, terrorism can work when a government deems acceptance of the terrorist demands, even considering the effect of acquiescence on the frequency of future demands, as far less onerous than the ongoing campaign of terror.

NATIONS WHOSE POPULATIONS ARE ALREADY SEVERELY DIVIDED AGAINST EACH OTHER
One factor is of greater importance than any other in predicting the consequences of political violence, the likely durability of a terrorist campaign, and the helpful or harmful effects of the steps the govern-

ment may take. That factor is the extent to which the terrorists' cause is sympathetic to a sizeable, disaffected portion of the population in the place where they are operating. When a society is already dangerously divided, terrorism can do great damage and is likely to be resistant to government efforts—far more than in relatively healthy democracies that enjoy strong support across the broad spectrum of their populations. Fortunately, the United States is not a severely divided society with regard to any present domestic or foreign terrorist threat. Still, it is worth pausing to look at the risks faced by countries such as Israel, Northern Ireland, and Spain.

No extended explanation is necessary for the increased difficulties of capturing the members of a terrorist group or preventing their violent actions in a situation where sizeable numbers of a population sympathize with their cause. At a minimum, law enforcement will find it far harder to get information about what occurs among people and in areas sympathetic to the terrorists. Beyond this, the terrorists will find it far easier to secure communications channels, physical facilities, money, and recruits. This is particularly true when the societal divisions are not purely political but are also ethnic, religious, or racial, pulling on deep strands of group loyalty that rival national allegiance.

What is less obvious is how terrorist acts can affect the familiar dynamics of transition from a secure, multi-ethnic society into a dangerously divided society characterized by high levels of violence, hatred, and mistrust among ethnic groups. The steps of this process can be encouraged and accelerated by targeted political violence such as we have seen in Northern Ireland, Israel, Sri Lanka, and Bosnia. A dangerously divided society is thus, for many separatist groups, a promising stage on the way to a separate national government, and terrorism can force the pace of this dangerous transition.

How then does terrorism change the dynamics of social division? First, although ethnic tensions escalate into hatreds and then violence between members of opposing groups even without the encouragement of terrorists, the process can be speeded by terrorist attacks on an opposing group, inviting tit-for-tat responses and fanning the flames of hatred and fear. This was long common in

Northern Ireland and in Israel. Indeed, retribution by members of the victim group against innocent members of the group from which the terrorists come—one of the most divisive of actions—is likely to be seen, mistakenly, as a deterrent to the terrorist attacks.

Second, a cycle of intergroup violence makes it difficult for members of either group to occupy a middle ground of tolerance and understanding. Even moderates may come to need an intense ethnic solidarity to remain secure, and the more violent members of each ethnic group are the natural leaders in providing that security. These processes can even be speeded by terrorists secretly attacking members of their own group. The process continues with increasing segregation of frightened ethnic communities. With this, prejudice grows and rumors are accepted as truth. Fewer members of either group find it comfortable to urge understanding of the other.

Third, each group will seek to bring the government to its side. The government may try to remain "neutral," but even the most natural steps—such as focusing investigation on the members of Group A if an attack was directed at a group they hate—are likely to solidify divisions, create deep distrust, and invite attacks on government security forces that can add a whole new dimension to the cycle of violence.

Accompanying all these forces are several others that sometimes produce still more threats. The group less favored by the government may turn to foreign enemies of the government for support. Others in the population may become less and less willing to consider ameliorative measures demanded by a besieged but combative portion of the population. Terrorist groups are likely to begin policing and enforcing their own demands on members of their ethnic group.

All of these paths towards hatred, fear, and division can be greased by the acts of even a few terrorists. The assassination of a leader of the opposition, an attack on one's own group falsely attributed to others, the killing of moderate rivals for leadership of a particular group, and attacks on law enforcement authorities—all of these can play major roles in speeding the dissolution of a multiethnic society. Thus, such societies are the most promising setting for important political "successes" for that form of violent politics accessible to even small groups—terrorism.

WHERE THE DAMAGE OF TERRORISM IS UNUSUALLY GREAT COMPARED TO THE
COSTS AND RISKS OF GIVING IN TO THE TERRORISTS' DEMANDS
Understanding the relative costs to the government of giving in and of holding out is also critical to understanding the contest which terrorism is all about. The violent group's demands of the government determine in part how likely the government is to give in—only "in part" because giving in once will likely encourage further demands by this group or others using the same threat of violence. Moreover, looking at the contest from the terrorist side, the terrorist group is likely to hold together and pursue its course longer if it sees its prospects for success as substantial. It will see them as substantial if it believes that the cost of political violence to the government far exceeds the costs to the government of compliance with the terrorists' demands, even when the government takes into account the likelihood of encouraging future terrorist demands.

The simple fact is that a handful of people can use murder, arson, and kidnapping to create public concerns strong enough and widely enough held to affect the policies and politics of the United States in ways totally disproportionate to their numbers, but far less because of the damage they can actually impose than because of its psychological, political, and social effects.

Some explanations of the great psychological impact of the limited damage generally caused by terrorism are helpful. As a start, social scientists have noted that people give far more weight to events that are vivid.[6] We do not have to search far for what makes terrorist acts "vivid." They are particularly frightening because terrorists purposely kill or maim otherwise uninvolved citizens. They also deprive us of a safeguard, neutrality, which we normally consider sufficient for our safety: the protection obtained by avoiding active or prominent involvement on either side in situations of conflict. A further explanation for the great psychological impact of terrorism is that terrorist attacks *seem* to present an immediate as well as violent challenge to the existing governmental structure of order and authority and may herald the prospect of escalating disorder and a forcible change in government.

What costs can a terrorist group actually impose on a relatively healthy and stable democracy such as ours? For the United States, terrorism does not pose any great national security threat to our stability or well-being as a nation—unless the traditional reluctance of terrorists to use weapons of mass destruction changes. With a single bomb, the terrorists in Oklahoma City killed as many people as die in homicides in three ordinary days in the entire United States. That is terrible, but even such an immense explosion represents far too small a percentage change in the annual violent death rate in the United States to be considered a threat to the nation as a whole.

Terrorism is, of course, a threat to public order that the national government must address. There is a real risk of the death of some citizens each year. If unpunished, terrorism can also encourage a spread of political violence by imitation as radical political groups compete for public attention or as others attempt to deal with the danger through forms of vigilantism. Psychologically, there is likely to be widespread fear, totally disproportionate to the actual danger, causing changes in economic and social behavior such as people avoiding air travel or downtown stores, or arming themselves unnecessarily.

National politics are also affected. Terrorism has an immense capacity to capture public attention, to cause otherwise ignored issues (such as the U.S. policy in the Middle East or at Waco) to displace others on a national agenda, and to make a few previously anonymous terrorists into relatively major participants in a political debate that would otherwise relegate them to very marginal roles. More fundamentally, terrorism threatens the domestic support for a government whose citizens consider their security its first obligation. Especially because politically motivated violence openly challenges the state's right to a monopoly of the use of force, a sense that the government is ineffective at keeping people safe from those who challenge the state's legitimacy can seriously undermine confidence, generating fear, disrespect, even ridicule. It is costly for a government to look impotent when being challenged so directly in its capacity to protect citizens.

All this is compounded by fears of international repercussions. An apparent inability to deal with an open challenge to the power and legitimacy of the government may make a nation look like a less strong and trustworthy ally.

What costs of giving in prevent a government from buying off the terrorist group? In some cases, the terrorist group is asking far too much, when the alternative is bearing the limited costs of terrorism until the group's members can be found, tried, and locked away. Israel would not, for example, comply with any demand that would significantly endanger its national security in order to end terrorist violence, which has never killed as many Israelis as traffic accidents do. Germany, Italy, and France had no adequate reason to change their forms of government to the satisfaction of the Red Army Faction, the Red Brigades, or Direct Action.

Terrorists can anticipate success only if what they are asking is of relatively minor importance to a strong and stable government. For example, the United States left Lebanon as a result of the bombing of the Marine barracks on October 23, 1983, and it secretly sold TOW anti-tank missiles to Iran in 1986 for use against Iraq in the hope of obtaining the release of a handful of American hostages, using the proceeds of the sale to support anti-Sandinista forces in Nicaragua. France promised, at about the same time, to obtain a very short sentence for a terrorist, Georges Ibrahim Abdallah, in order to end a bombing spree on his behalf. Even in such cases, governments must consider seriously the impact of giving in on future political demands and, to a lesser extent, on their relationships with other nations: allies may find them weak or untrustworthy in a shared battle against particular forms of political violence, or—in the case of the U.S. sale of missiles to Iran—hypocritical. So even making deals, as in these three cases, generally makes sense only if the capitulation can be sufficiently obscured. That hope and expectation lay behind the government action in each of these examples.

If the government concludes that the costs of giving in to terrorist demands are too high, compared to the expected cost of political violence until the group can be caught and dismantled, the terrorist group may try to raise these costs either by escalating the damage from individual attacks or by showing an ability and a willingness to continue a course of violence over months or years or even decades. Even with purely conventional terrorist weapons, the Provisional IRA in Northern Ireland and the Palestine Liberation Organization in the Middle East had the capacity and tenacity to continue a costly terrorist campaign, wearing down the willingness of both Britain and Israel to continue to bear the costs, and building the prospect that the violence would continue for a very long period. The negotiations that have resulted in Northern Ireland and the Middle East surely reflect some success of these strategies. But in both situations, the contest between the government and the violent groups took place in the only truly dangerous setting for resisting terrorism: a society already severely divided along racial, religious, or ethnic lines.

Chapter 2

The Special Problems Presented by International Terrorism

The problems of prosecution, prevention, and intelligence-gathering that always characterize efforts to deal with terrorism are magnified when the terrorist organization can use foreign territory or even a foreign state to assist its operations. The difficulties presented by the availability of foreign territory for relatively safe organizing activities, support gathering, and operations are the subject of this and the next two chapters. (The further complexities when a state sponsors and supports terrorism, and the issues surrounding a military response by the United States, are the subject of Chapter 5.)

A single case, the 1985 hijacking of the Italian cruise liner, the *Achille Lauro*, provides a vivid introduction to three sets of problems created by terrorist use of foreign territory. First, the rules and opportunities for intelligence-gathering are greatly affected by the fact that the information is sought abroad, a matter this chapter explores in some detail with a description of the seizure of the *Achille Lauro*, and the steps that followed in the United States, Italy, and Egypt.

Second, as to prevention, the steps the United States would like to take to protect Americans abroad depend upon the cooperation of foreign governments. This is most vivid when the subject is the rescue of hostages or of a hijacked plane or ship. (I return to hostage situations in Chapter 3.) Third, as to arrest, trial, and punishment, international law flatly forbids employing U.S. security forces—law enforcement or military—in a foreign country without the consent of that country. The breach of that prohibition has dramatic conse-quences in the story that follows. (So it is important to explore the mechanisms and limits of international cooperation when a violent group uses foreign territory in some way as it targets American citizens. That is the task of Chapter 4.)

The Hijacking of the Achille Lauro

At about 1:00 P.M. on Monday, October 7, 1985, a radio station in Sweden picked up an emergency message from the captain of the Italian cruise liner, the *Achille Lauro*, announcing that the ship had been hijacked by a group of armed men as it left Alexandria, Egypt, on the sixth day of a twelve-day Mediterranean cruise. That evening the hijackers, who described themselves as members of the Palestin-ian Liberation Front (PLF), demanded that Israel release a group of 50 Palestinian prisoners. Otherwise, the hijackers would execute hostages, starting with American passengers. They threatened to blow up the liner if anyone attempted a rescue effort.

International terrorism and acts such as this were not new to the United States. A few months before, Palestinian terrorists had hi-jacked TWA Flight 847 in Europe and held the passengers hostage in Beirut. An American had been murdered; the hijackers escaped. Thus, arrangements for crisis management of terrorist incidents in the United States were well in place. The U.S. interagency crisis team, called the Operational Sub-Group (OSG), had as its lead agency the National Security Council (NSC) and was headed by the deputy director of the NSC staff, Vice Admiral John M. Poindexter. The group included representatives of the State Department, the Defense Department, the CIA, the FBI, and the White House. Its recommen-dations went to President Ronald Reagan through the national secu-rity advisor, Robert McFarlane.

The Italians estimated that there were only ten to fourteen U.S. citizens on board when the ship was hijacked; the rest were touring in Egypt. But soon the ship's location became a mystery. It sailed north from Egypt into international waters, having turned off its radio signals, thus eliminating one major source of information to United States and allied intelligence agencies. U.S., Italian, and

British reconnaissance aircraft could not find it in the crowded eastern Mediterranean.

The United States had developed highly trained hostage rescue teams that operated under the Defense Department's Joint Special Operations Command (JSOC). Now the Operational Sub-Group of the National Security Council moved quickly to put them to use. These teams, including a group of specially trained Navy divers known as SEAL (Sea, Air, Land) Team 6, flew to Sicily under the command of Brigadier General Carl Stiner. Meanwhile, the United States urged friendly governments to keep the ship in international waters, both to avoid legal objections to a rescue effort carried out without the consent of neighboring nations, and to prevent a repeat of the difficulties that followed the 1985 hijacking of TWA Flight 847 when rescue operations were frustrated after hostages had been scattered to various locations throughout Beirut. (See Chapter 3.)

The rescue plan and its use of JSOC capabilities reflected two U.S. priorities: to show American citizens and their allies abroad that the United States was not a "paper tiger" in dealing with terrorists, and to demonstrate to would-be terrorists that terrorism against the United States would not pay. The confidence and pride of American citizens was at stake; so was the sense of American determination in confronting political violence. That meant that the United States would not negotiate with the terrorists under any circumstances, and it also meant using the formidable U.S. military capabilities.

The Italian government, which had also organized itself for the crisis, had very different priorities. Its foreign policy required it to maintain very close relations with the Arab states and the PLO. More broadly, it wanted to build and display its diplomatic influence as a Mediterranean power. And many more of its citizens were at risk, both on the *Achille Lauro* now and, in future months, in Italy itself, if Italy's response stimulated increased terrorism on its soil. So, Italian officials were quickly in touch with PLO leader Yasir Arafat and the leaders of other Arab states, including those that had sponsored terrorist attacks in the past.

Negotiations were strongly favored by the Italian government of Prime Minister Bettino Craxi. A military rescue assault was strongly favored by the United States. Which was preferable in terms of lives and principle depended not only on national priorities but also on the likely consequences, which in turn depended on who was responsible for the hijacking and why. The director of central intelligence (who is also the head of the CIA) has leadership responsibility for a number of agencies that form the "intelligence community" of the United States. Three of these agencies—the CIA, the Defense Intelligence Agency (DIA), and the Bureau of Intelligence and Research in the State Department (INR)—each had a different answer to this question. The hijackers had identified themselves as members of the Palestinian Liberation Front (PLF), but that organization had split into three groups with widely divergent allegiances. One faction was loyal to Yasir Arafat; another, extremely hostile to Arafat, was supported by Syria; and a third, also opposed to Arafat, was supported by Libya.

Since the PLO and Arafat greatly valued Italian and Egyptian friendship, the CIA and the DIA believed the hijacking of an Italian ship from Egyptian waters could not have been carried out by the PLF group loyal to Arafat. It "made sense" that it would be carried out by a group trying to disrupt the peace feelers that Arafat, even then, was making toward Israel and the West. In contrast, the State Department's INR thought that the hijackers came from the faction loyal to Arafat, and explained the hijacking as almost accidental, a mistake by panicked terrorists who had simply wanted to ride the *Achille Lauro* to its next destination in Israel for attacks in that country. But those in the State Department responsible for diplomacy—and thus for the peace process—refused to accept INR's conclusions, as they seemed to threaten budding U.S. relations with Arafat.

Intelligence can be extremely important, even if sometimes unwelcome. If INR was right, the hijackers did not really want the *Achille Lauro* or its passengers, so negotiations would be very likely to succeed, and there was little point in trying to teach a lesson on this occasion. If the CIA or the DIA was right, negotiations would be unlikely to succeed—at least without major concessions—and concerns about both national strategy in dealing with terrorism and the safety of passengers dictated a military rescue effort.

As the hours and days wore on, more and more signs indicated that INR was right. In particular, by Thursday Israeli intelligence sources had picked up communications that very strongly suggested that the hijackers were connected to the PLF faction headed by Abu Abbas, which is within the PLO and loyal to Yasir Arafat.

Meanwhile, the possibility of a rescue without diplomatic complications became moot when the *Achille Lauro* made its way into Egyptian waters. After a futile effort by the hijackers to obtain some concessions from Israel in exchange for releasing the ship, and then another effort, resisted by the United States, to obtain guarantees of safety from the United States, Great Britain, and Germany, the terrorists negotiated the release of the ship and their own freedom with the Egyptians and appeared on live television holding up victory signs as an Egyptian patrol boat took them to a cheering group of bystanders in Port Said.

Italian Prime Minister Craxi had agreed to their release without, he later said somewhat implausibly, knowing that they had murdered a wheelchair-bound American, Leon Klinghoffer, during the days they were in control of the ship. The public release of this fact shortly after the remaining hostages were released turned a triumph of Italian diplomacy into an occasion of bitter recriminations by the United States. The United States demanded extradition of the four hijackers for trial in the United States. President Hosni Mubarak of Egypt said that they had already left Egypt. In fact, they were still in Egypt as the U.S. crisis team and its informal contact with Israel, Colonel Oliver North, learned from Israeli intelligence through Israel's military attaché in Washington. The United States confirmed this through electronic surveillance carried out by another member of the U.S. intelligence community.

Colonel North then proposed to Admiral Poindexter that the United States force down, safely in Sicily, the Egyptian plane that was going to spirit away the four hijackers and their two leaders, the senior PLF-PLO official, Abu Abbas, who had negotiated the end of the hijacking, and Hani Al-Hassan, a close aide to Yasir Arafat. With the aid of Israeli and U.S. intelligence, the flight was spotted and forced by U.S. fighters to land in Sicily.

A Short Interruption: Covert Gathering of Information

U.S. intelligence relies on four "networks" for gathering information abroad. Two are highly expensive technical networks: photo reconnaissance and the interception of radio and other signals. The use the United States was able to make of these in the *Achille Lauro* case is unusual for intelligence-gathering about terrorists. The other two "networks" are much more important for that purpose: human agents and liaison with foreign intelligence organizations.

Almost every Western democracy assigns responsibility for gathering information abroad to different organizations from those operating at home. In the United States, the Federal Bureau of Investigation is responsible for counterintelligence operations and investigations carried on within the borders of the United States. The CIA is primarily responsible for intelligence collection abroad, sharing this responsibility with other members of the intelligence community. Thus, the FBI led the investigations of the World Trade Center and Oklahoma City bombings, while the CIA played a central role in 1995 in Southern Asia in the hunt for and capture of Ramzi Yousef, the mastermind behind the World Trade Center bombings, as well as in the 1997 capture of Mir Aimal Kansi, accused of killing several persons at the front gates of CIA headquarters (see discussion below). Germany's counterpart organizations are, respectively, the Bureau for the Protection of the Constitution (BfV) and the Military Intelligence Service (MAD). The British intelligence organizations, MI-5 and MI-6, divide responsibilities in similar fashion.

GATHERING INTELLIGENCE ON TERRORISTS ABROAD

Major U.S. investigations abroad involving foreign-based terrorist groups and attacks on Americans abroad are generally conducted by a joint task force under the leadership of the State Department and including the Department of Justice. One such case was the investigation of the bombing of Pan Am Flight 103 over Lockerbie, Scotland. Since the same terrorist group may operate in several countries, and several organizations from each nation may have relevant responsibilities, there are often overlapping interests, and a number of investigative agencies may need to cooperate.

A primary objective of intelligence acquisition abroad is to anticipate the action of terrorist groups. Information must be acquired about the group's capabilities, its location, and whether it is supported by important groups in a particular country. The history of its acts and its statements will tell something of its purposes and its modus operandi. From information about capability, location, support, intention, and habitual conduct, the object is to define the group's objectives clearly enough to guess what it might do next (thus suggesting steps aimed at prevention and capture).

Much overseas intelligence involves the careful analysis of materials that are made available by local police abroad, foreign intelligence agencies, or foreign ministry agencies, or that are public documents. Embassies of countries threatened by a terrorist group maintain contact with the police and other officials in any nation where the group is operating. Newspaper accounts are studied, and the speeches and travels of suspected terrorists and those closely related to them are analyzed.

Terrorist groups are, in the vernacular of intelligence, a "hard target," meaning that sophisticated, technical means of information gathering are not generally helpful. Satellite photos can show the presence of a training camp but they will not reveal the purpose of the people there: even the physical features of military training camps and terrorist training camps are virtually identical. Means of overhearing electronic communications have been helpful in some cases, such as the capture of the hijackers of the *Achille Lauro*, but this, too, is relatively rare. In that case significant conclusions about the identity of the terrorists were derived from monitoring their communications with Abu Abbas's faction of the PLF, and the fact that they remained in Egypt after President Mubarak said that they had left was confirmed by electronic intelligence. Under ordinary circumstances the use of telephone taps or bugs in a country with which we have a close liaison relationship would only be carried out with the consent and cooperation of local authorities; although no U.S. law requires this, international law and diplomacy both do.

Human sources are the best possible source about the activities and plans of a terrorist group, and one's own agent (typically a foreign national) infiltrated into a terrorist group would be the most reliable human source. Unfortunately, the headquarters of a terrorist group is likely to be in a place where U.S. intelligence officers would find it hard to develop and place agents. Moreover, as with domestic terrorist groups, the members have often known each other for very long periods and do not accept strangers as new members. Finally, many terrorist groups require a new member to commit a serious crime, a matter that may cause the intelligence agency to balk. American support for a killing, even abroad, is illegal and plainly unacceptable.

One common human source is a "walk-in" to a U.S. diplomatic facility or to a friendly government agency, who may simply feel that he is in over his head, or hope to be paid for information, or even want to damage a rival, violent group. The trouble is that such walk-ins are frequently unreliable. The person may be a con artist or simply expressing political or personal biases on the basis of inadequate information. More serious, he may have been sent as a provocation or to learn more about the intelligence agency's processes: to identify its officers, its operating style, or its physical security.

Still, such volunteered information can be crucial. For example, in 1997, the CIA successfully concluded a four-year search for the man who had used an AK-47 to kill two CIA employees outside the agency's headquarters in Langley, Virginia. Mir Aimal Kansi had fled to Afghanistan and Pakistan where his family and clan could provide protection. The United States responded by offering a $2 million reward for information leading to Kansi's arrest, and it publicized the reward through posters, newspaper ads, and tens of thousands of matchbooks showing Kansi's photograph. As a result, individuals whose identities have been kept secret walked in, identified, and located Kansi to get the reward. The informants even convinced Kansi to come to a place where a specially trained FBI team could arrest him. There, with the agreement of the government of Pakistan, U.S. agents put him on a plane to the United States for trial.

The other major category of agents is those individuals who want a reduced sentence for unrelated criminal conduct. Some experts believe that law enforcement agencies such as Scotland Yard's Special Branch in Britain have a great advantage over strictly intelligence-gathering agencies such as Britain's MI-5 in developing informants, for most informants have been found among those who have been arrested and threatened with punishment for other crimes. The capacity to create pressure and to make deals in these circumstances gives law enforcement agencies leverage that intelligence agencies lack. Benefiting from such leverage abroad requires cooperation with foreign police agencies.

As in the case of domestic gathering of information about secret terrorist groups, most of the information arrives in small, isolated pieces. Even informants may know just a little about a particular individual's travel plans, say, or an unusual purchase of explosives or the aliases of another. Putting the pieces together in a coherent and timely manner is much of the challenge in the intelligence collection process. For the United States, it requires unusual levels of trust and sharing among foreign and domestic intelligence and law enforcement organizations.

THE APPLICABLE RULES

Law, executive orders, and other rules are also part of the complex environment for intelligence-gathering about foreign groups. In the United States, the rights of individuals under intelligence rules and, correspondingly, the limitations under which intelligence activities are undertaken depend upon whether the victim is, on the one hand, a citizen or a resident or, on the other, has no substantial ties to the United States, and upon whether the investigation takes place within the United States or elsewhere. There are very few rules with regard to actions taken by a U.S. intelligence agency abroad against someone who is neither a U.S. citizen nor a resident alien, and these are generally applicable to covert operations, not intelligence-gathering.

One of the few flat prohibitions followed revelations in the 1970s to the Church Committee of the U.S. Senate that the CIA had attempted to kill Cuban President Fidel Castro. Congress and the president came to an agreement now embodied in Executive Order 12333 that assassinations by U.S. agencies were absolutely prohibited. Few other such flat prohibitions apply to intelligence agencies operating abroad and dealing with foreign nationals; political restraints based on public opinion and the risk of discovery are all that buttress what is in general a structure of review and oversight, not rules and prohibitions.

For other activities, the system in the United States works like this. Under Executive Order 12333, each of the agencies in the U.S. intelligence community must adopt written procedures specifying what their agents can do and must submit these procedures to the attorney general. Although the procedures are classified, it is known that they are generally in the form of process requirements, not absolute prohibitions. They are largely designed in terms of accountability, requiring higher and higher levels of approval for more and more dangerous or questionable actions. The effect is to require both that more people must agree and that those who give final approval be more publicly accountable.

Each U.S. intelligence agency is also required to have regular procedures for reporting to those executive and congressional bodies with oversight responsibility any serious crimes against U.S. law committed by any intelligence agent or cooperating individual. In connection with this duty to report unlawful activity, the inspectors general and the general counsel of each intelligence agency must be given full access to agency records. If the matter is very secret, the report may go directly to the attorney general. Occasionally, intelligence agencies seek the approval of the Department of Justice before an operation.

All this applies both to normal intelligence-gathering and to covert operations to disrupt a terrorist group. An additional set of procedures also covers the latter: in the United States, a multi-departmental committee (at the level of deputy department heads) with Department of Justice representation is convened to review proposed covert actions abroad before they are submitted to a cabinet committee and then for the legally required, personal approval of the president. Legislation also provides for congressional oversight of such CIA operations.

The involvement of the attorney general or deputy attorney general is required at many points of this decision-making process to ensure concern for certain values and legal norms that might otherwise be ignored. An office within the Department of Justice specializes in following, and advising on, these matters. But exactly what values the Department of Justice is protecting is unclear; there is very little law that is directly applicable. The three clearest bases for the attorney general to object to an action are that American citizens are involved and that there is no convincing justification for the intelligence measure; that the activity being proposed threatens freedoms protected by the First Amendment of the U.S. Constitution; or that the operation violates human rights.

A second form of regulatory control is exerted by the executive in the form of the President's Intelligence Oversight Board (PIOB). The PIOB is responsible for monitoring intelligence activities and reviewing agency procedures. It reports to the president and forwards reports of illegal activity to the attorney general.

A final form of regulatory control is oversight by the Intelligence Committees of the House and the Senate. Covert actions are to be reported to them in advance if possible; if not, then after the fact. (In the Iran-Contra affair, executive officials were accused of illegally circumventing this requirement.) The president must also provide a classified report of all electronic surveillance of international terrorists in the United States done under the Foreign Intelligence Surveillance Act, and the Committees are told of every intelligence search that is conducted under similar powers. More general requirements specify that the Committees be kept fully informed in the intelligence area.

Of course, all oversight depends upon the willingness of CIA officers in the field to keep their superiors, the local U.S. ambassador, and Congress informed. CIA Director John Deutch tried to make that obligation clear in the fall of 1995 when he disciplined a number of officers formerly stationed in Guatemala. They had withheld information that one of their sources, a Guatemalan military officer, had been involved in the murder of a U.S. citizen as well as the killing of the Guatemalan husband of another U.S. citizen. Deutch fired two senior officials, demoted another, and reprimanded seven others for suppressing information or for failing to supervise operations for which they were responsible. In contrast, in 1984 Israel acted in an opposite way when the prime minister sharply reprimanded those who brought him unwanted information of misdeeds by Shin Bet (the General Security Service). That strategy is extremely dangerous to democratic values, because it is designed to prevent oversight and to deny accountability to the public.[1]

Back to the Sigonella Airbase in Sicily

There is an important lesson in the unwinding of the Achille Lauro story. With the hostages now freed by Wednesday, October 9, 1985, the United States turned its attention to capturing and punishing the terrorists and their leaders. But when an international event takes place abroad, these steps require the cooperation of allies and that, in turn, is likely to depend upon compliance with international law. The United States had ignored that in bringing down an Egyptian airliner and was to disregard Italian sovereignty as well. The results reflected the constraints that diplomacy and international law impose in dealing with terrorists abroad.

The Italians had only been notified at the last moment of the plan to bring the Egyptian plane down on Italian territory. Even then, Prime Minister Craxi was not informed of the rest of the plan, which was to have General Stiner's JSOC team arrive simultaneously, surround the plane, forcibly remove the four terrorists and their two superiors, and put them on a waiting plane for immediate flight to the United States and trial.

Thus it was to the surprise and outrage of Italian officials that the forced landing of the Egyptian plane at Sigonella, a NATO airbase on Sicily, was accompanied by the landing of two C-141 troop transports. Fifty heavily armed U.S. troops emerged from the planes and rushed to surround the Egyptian aircraft. They were immediately confronted by a contingent of about 50 Italian soldiers and police, who also surrounded the Egyptian plane. When U.S. troops positioned fuel trucks to prevent the Egyptian plane from taking off, Italian troops, in turn, moved heavy machinery to block the American planes.

Over one hundred heavily armed U.S. and Italian troops stood facing each other while their commanders engaged in a prolonged shouting match.

The Americans had hoped to remove the hijackers and their leaders without the consent of the Italian government, which had not been informed of the plan. That would have left Italy free to protest U.S. actions and deny responsibility for seizure of an Egyptian plane and the capture of the hijackers and their leaders. But Italy defended its own sovereignty over the Sigonella airbase, and now there was confrontation.

International law is important, at least in dealings among friendly nations. It sets basic standards of conduct, and the United States was departing from them on this occasion as it followed Oliver North's plan. Very quickly Italian newspapers challenged this, and rejected the legality of the interception of an Egyptian civilian aircraft. Mass protests by Egyptian students at the American University in Cairo were even more dramatic evidence of the political power of international law among friends. Had the raid been traceable to a PLF faction controlled by Libya, the United States might well have responded with aerial attacks on Libya without any great concern over whether they constituted "self defense," which is legal under international law, or "reprisal," which is forbidden by the UN Charter. But Italy was an ally and Egypt a friend.

President Reagan called Prime Minister Craxi and eventually agreed that the U.S. force would "stand down," leaving it to Italy to take custody of the four hijackers and the two Palestinian emissaries. U.S. newspapers and political leaders celebrated a rare triumph in the war against terrorism.

The Italians removed the four hijackers from the Egyptian airplane without difficulty, but Abbas and Hassan claimed diplomatic immunity as envoys of Yasir Arafat, and the Egyptian government insisted that the plane itself, on a special governmental mission, enjoyed diplomatic immunity under international law. The claims of the emissaries and of the government of Egypt had to be taken seriously by Prime Minister Craxi and his government. Good relations with the Arab governments that shared the Mediterranean with Italy were at the crux of Italy's foreign policy. Italy could expect terrorist attacks on its own territory or people if it seized Abbas and Hassan. Moreover, Egypt was continuing to hold the *Achille Lauro* along with its largely Italian crew of several hundred.

The United States then sought extradition of Abbas and the others. Congress had passed a statute making it a crime against the United States to take a U.S. citizen hostage anywhere in the world. International law was unclear on the validity of such extraterritorial jurisdiction, but a very strong argument could be made for it under the widely accepted right of any state to protect itself from foreign-based attacks. After all, Americans were targeted simply because they were Americans.

A nation that has been requested to extradite someone within its territory generally sends the matter first to its judges for a determination of whether the available extradition treaties apply. That was certainly the standard procedure in Italy. Only after a judicial decision has been reached does the political arm of government decide whether the extradition should be allowed. At that stage, political concerns about retaliation and foreign policy are likely to be important, although they are often masked behind legal technicalities or the broad exception in extradition treaties for "political offenses." But here the Italian government bypassed the judicial stage and quickly rejected a U.S. request to extradite Abu Abbas. Prime Minister Craxi later explained that "the request for the provisional arrest [pending extradition] though formally correct, did not, in the Justice Minister's opinion, satisfy the factual and substantive requirements laid down by Italian law."[2]

In the meantime, Italy had moved the Egyptian plane with its two passengers from the NATO base in Sicily to Rome. The flight was shadowed by USOC General Stiner in a training jet, but since the United States had neither sought nor received permission for that flight in Italian airspace, the Italian government again protested loudly to the U.S. Embassy. The United States had again disregarded Italian sovereignty.

The Craxi government decided to allow the Egyptian plane to depart to Yugoslavia with its two important passengers. The United States reacted in outrage, the U.S. ambassador, Maxwell Rabb, stating that "the U.S. government finds it incomprehensible that Italian authorities permitted Abu Abbas to leave Italy despite a U.S. government request for his arrest and detention."[3] It said that the United States was "astonished and disappointed at this breach of any reasonable standard of due process."[4] The White House said that President Reagan felt "personally betrayed" by Prime Minister Craxi's decision.

This presented the occasion for the Italian Republican Party, one of the parties that formed the coalition behind Prime Minister Craxi, to withdraw, causing Craxi's government to fall. The United States hardly wanted this, for it created a new opening for the Communist Party of Italy to seek to join a governing coalition. President Reagan therefore wrote to Bettino Craxi on October 19, eight days after the strange events at Sigonella Airbase, reminding his "friend Bettino" that "despite [recent] differences, which we have dealt with in a frank and friendly way, we share fundamental commitments on the necessity to respond with firmness to the threat of international terrorism. . . . Italian-American relations have been and will remain wide, deep and solid, and I am sure that our personal relationship will continue to be firmly tied to this tradition."[5]

Eight months later, an Italian court imposed stiff sentences on three of the hijackers. Abu Abbas received a life sentence in absentia. (By the end of 1996, all three hijackers had "escaped" while on leave from Italian prison.)

Conclusion

The story of the *Achille Lauro* hijacking is a reminder of both the possibility and the limits of unilateral action by the United States, as a world superpower. The United States cannot defy international law in dealing with its allies or other nations with which it wants to cooperate. It can use the influence created by its military, diplomatic, and economic resources to elicit cooperation, within limits, even from nations who see their own self-interest in avoiding conflict with a terrorist group.

More than self-interest may be involved. Italy did not share the attitudes of the United States toward the hijackers of the *Achille Lauro* nor the view of its powerful ally as to how best to address such situations. With different interests, different capabilities, and different strategies, the problem of working together to deal with a terrorist event is a difficult one even for two very friendly nations.

For either Italy or the United States to decide what was in its best interest, it needed strategic intelligence about the various groups that might be responsible for seizing the *Achille Lauro*. That intelligence can come from extremely sophisticated technology, from human agents, or from liaison with friendly nations. To carry out a rescue operation, a nation needs tactical intelligence as well. The bringing down of the Egyptian airliner carrying the terrorists would not have been possible without substantial information about its flight. Rescuing the hostages while the *Achille Lauro* was at sea was impossible because that information was lacking. Plainly maintaining the capacity to gather and process intelligence abroad is critical to dealing with terrorist events outside the United States.

Chapter 3

Hostage and Other Negotiations

Early on the morning of June 14, 1985, C.E. Meyer, then president of Trans World Airlines, was awakened by a telephone call from the TWA operational planning group at New York's John F. Kennedy International Airport, the department responsible for scheduling and tracking the airline's worldwide movements. He was told that TWA's daily flight from Athens to Rome, Flight 847, had been hijacked several minutes after takeoff. The airliner, a Boeing 727, was seized by two Lebanese members of the radical Shi'ite Muslim Hezbollah sect armed with a .45 caliber pistol and hand grenades. They had threatened to kill all the passengers and blow up the plane if their demands were not met. Their most prominent demand was the release of 766 Shi'ite prisoners held in Israel since their capture during Israel's recent occupation of southern Lebanon.

Israel had earlier expressed an intention to release the prisoners "as the security situation in southern Lebanon permitted."[1] None had been charged or convicted of a crime. All were held in preventive detention for fear of future terrorist activities.

Before the crisis was over, one hostage, a U.S. Navy diver named Robert Stethem, was brutalized and then murdered by the hijackers at an early stop in Beirut, while the plane was in the course of two days of constant movement between Lebanon and Algeria. When it finally settled in Beirut, most of the hostages were put in the hands of armed militiamen from the less radical Amal faction that exercised much of such control as there was in Beirut. Thereafter, they were held in various locations in and around Beirut for the remainder of their seventeen-day captivity in order to thwart a rescue mission.

The Reagan administration first briefly considered using the Air Force's specially trained Delta Force to free the hostages, a plan that was thwarted by the constant movement of the TWA plane and the eventual dispersion of the hostages. Delta Force did not move as quickly as it might have, taking 24 hours to assemble the right equipment and get 400 people airborne. Allies were less than helpful. Italy delayed granting permission for Delta Force to land at the NATO airbase in Sigonella. Non-allied Arab nations were not helpful at all; Algeria made clear that it would not tolerate any U.S. military action in Algerian territory and declined to keep the TWA plane on the ground when it was there.

Turning then to negotiations, President Reagan's team announced that it had decided immediately not to agree to any "linkage" between the release of the TWA hostages and the release of the Shi'ite prisoners in Israel. On the other hand, it was happy to "encourage" Israel to make the release, once the hostages were freed. Israel, in turn, repeated its willingness to free the Shi'ite prisoners it held, but only at the official request of the U.S. government.

The U.S. negotiators thus saw their task as to encourage Israel to do what it was willing to do without making the Israeli action the explicit reward for taking and then releasing American hostages. This U.S. distinction was so fine that it must have escaped many observers and even the players themselves. Still, Syrian President Hafez al-Assad somehow was given a clear enough impression that the United States would press Israel for an early release of the Shi'ite prisoners to enable him to assure the leader of the Amal faction, Nabih Berri, that that would be the consequence if the hostages were permitted to leave Lebanon. U.S. statements that the terrorists "will be held to account" delayed the deal until Syrian authorities provided Hezbollah with assurances that no retaliation was planned.

Whatever assurances the United States gave in this respect did not, apparently, cover efforts to bring the murdering hijackers to justice. After the hostages were released, the United States offered rewards for the suspects, considered a plan to kidnap one of the hijackers, and made clear the legal authority for the CIA or the FBI to carry out arrests abroad. On January 13, 1987, one of the hijackers, Mohammed Ali Hammadei, was arrested at Frankfurt Airport and, after U.S. requests for extradition were denied, tried and convicted in Germany. Another terrorist, more marginally linked to the hijacking, was seized in a daring operation in international waters off Cyprus: Fawas Younis had been a guard during the hijacking while the plane was in Beirut and had later been involved in hijacking a Jordanian plane. He was tried and convicted in the United States.

Hostage-Taking as a Terrorist Tactic

Ariel Merari, a psychologist by profession, is one of Israel's top hostage negotiators.[2] I have learned from him the set of purposes, choices, factual variations, and lessons of history that govern when terrorists have taken hostages. It was from this menu that American and Italian decision-makers had to choose when confronted with the holding of hostages by PLF terrorists on the *Achille Lauro* and by Shi'ite terrorists on TWA Flight 847 and in Beirut.

As a tactic, hostage-taking has very clear advantages for a politically violent group. I noted in Chapter 1 that terrorism is best understood as an effort to speak to audiences with a greatly amplified voice. Duration is as important as volume for conveying a message and creating the public concerns that can move the government. Holding hostages keeps the story in the lead of television news and on the front pages of newspapers throughout the country for a far more sustained period of time than any terrorist action except a far more difficult extended campaign of bombing. The holding of American hostages in Lebanon following the hijacking of TWA Flight 847 in 1985 captured the headlines for weeks. Even our largest corporations could not have afforded to buy similar access to the American people. Speaking of this hijacking, the State Department Legal Advisor Abraham Sofaer said, "The hijackers sought publicity, and they got it. The world was treated to a media extravaganza that gave irresponsibility and tastelessness a new meaning."[3] Tom Brokaw, NBC News anchor, and his ABC counterpart, Peter Jennings, agreed that the press had served the terrorists' purposes too well.

There is also something qualitatively different about hostage-taking. The story is more vivid and dramatic because the lives of ordinary Americans remain at stake. There is drama in the choice confronting the government between its responsibility to individual citizens and its responsibility to uphold its policies for discouraging terrorism. And demonstrating the powerlessness of the most powerful leaders in the world—one important purpose of taking hostages—is itself dramatic. To see this clearly, one need only consider the drama of the prolonged defiance of authority in non-hostage situations at Waco, Texas, or Ruby Ridge, Idaho, or Jordan, Montana.[4]

In other crucial ways, cases of hostage-taking are likely to differ. One dimension of differences, emphasized by Merari, depends on where the hostages are held. Kidnapping involves the taking of one or a few individuals to a secret location and making demands in exchange for their release. In 1978, terrorists of the left kidnapped Italy's Christian Democratic party leader, Aldo Moro, and hid him for a prolonged period before killing him. The TWA Flight 847 hostages were, for fifteen days, hidden in various places in the Beirut area. The fact that the location is secret prevents the use of an armed rescue assault. The kidnappers generally expect to escape before their location is discovered.

The location of hostage-takers and of the hostages is no secret under a second variation—barricade-hostage events. Here, the location is known and generally surrounded by security forces and the curious, but an armed assault by rescuers is deterred by the threat that the kidnappers will kill the hostages. Because it cannot hold out forever, the violent group must set deadlines for the meeting of its demands. This adds to the drama and to the pressure on government officials. One of the demands will inevitably be the free conduct of the hostage-takers to a place from which they can escape safely.

The hijacking of a plane or ship, using its passengers as hostages, is a third variation. While the vessel or plane is mobile, it may be ordered to a location friendly to the terrorists where an assault may be impossible. For example, an assault by American forces on the *Achille Lauro* became impossible when it moved into the territorial waters of Egypt; Delta Force could not be used to invade TWA Flight 847 when it was in Algiers or Deirut If the plane or ship is cornered in a country that will permit an armed assault, the situation becomes very much like a barricade-hostage event.

The Choices Available to the United States and the Factors that Bear upon Them

Confronted with a politically violent group that is making demands and threatening to kill hostages if the demands are not met, the United States has three options. First, it can negotiate in good faith with the group, making concessions if necessary to obtain the release of the hostages. Second, it can sometimes launch a rescue mission, using specially trained forces (like the military teams used abroad in the *Achille Lauro* case or the FBI's hostage rescue team for events taking place within the United States). Such risky operations have been stunningly successful when used by Israel at Entebbe and by Germany at Mogadishu.[5] On other occasions, they have led to considerable loss of life, even when carried out by superbly skilled Israeli forces. Twenty-one high school students were killed when Israeli forces stormed hostage-holding terrorists at Ma'alot in 1975.

The final option, stalling, may be successful in dealing with a bank robber who has taken hostages at the last minute by mistake or with terrorists who have not planned their hostage-taking, like those in the *Achille Lauro* case. But where the hostage-taking is purposeful and planned, stalling can be pursued for only a limited period in the hope of tiring and confusing the terrorists or of encouraging them to develop human bonds with those they hold.

A nation is wise to have a well-established strategy to guide its response to hostage-taking. Having a consistent policy avoids decision-making under extreme pressure, sometimes while confronted by the terrified relatives of the hostages. But beyond this, there are other real disadvantages to ad hoc responses. If the decision on a particular occasion is to refuse concessions, it would have been far wiser to let that be known before the hostages were taken. "No concessions" has been the announced policy of the United States for many years. If the policy is to negotiate concessions, it would be far wiser not to stake the nation's prestige on prior statements of firmness. For example, negotiating for the release of hostages held by Iranian-backed groups in Lebanon after having denounced any concessions by our allies made the Reagan administration look either foolish or duplicitous. But a clear policy need not be simple; Israel, as we will see, has adopted a more complicated "mixed" policy that depends upon certain obvious characteristics of the situation it confronts.

Choosing between a policy of negotiation and one of "no concessions"

The United States has an announced policy of "no concessions," but the choice is not an obvious one. There are advantages in the short term and in the long term to a strategy that makes concessions, just as there are to a "no concessions" policy.

Negotiating concessions minimizes the risk to the hostages in the short run. In the medium run, it also avoids the escalation of the particular conflict that can come from humiliating the attacking group or from killing or capturing its members. The last—capturing—is particularly important. When a terrorist leader is held in a national prison, the situation is ripe for the taking of further hostages in the hope of obtaining his release. Indeed, in the long run, the unwillingness of a nation to capitulate to demands made in exchange for the lives of a handful of hostages may lead to efforts to take larger and larger groups of hostages.

The short-term advantages of a policy of "no concessions" lie in public morale, government prestige, and increasing the possibilities of leading a united multinational confrontation with politically violent groups. The short-term benefits of firmness also include denying the terrorists the advantages they can get from payments of ransom money, such as the French seem to have made to obtain the release of hostages held by Iran. Equally advantageous to the terrorists are concessions in the form of a release of their imprisoned associates. Sometimes this is a bad bargain for the government: Ariel Merari estimates that dozens of Israeli citizens have been killed by the very prisoners released in exchange for the release of one or a very few Israeli hostages.

Still, it is the long-term advantages that argue most powerfully for a policy of firmness. A nation that makes concessions to violent groups that threaten the lives of hostages (or that make other threats) invites the same group and other groups to engage in the same tactics. Within two months after Germany released prisoners to the Red Army Faction (RAF) in 1975 in exchange for the release of Peter Lorenz, a mayoral candidate in West Berlin, it experienced new hostage-taking events in Stockholm and similar demands by the same group. This time, it refused to make concessions, and Sweden mounted a successful armed assault, and two years later, Germany again refused and instead attacked RAF terrorists who had seized a planeload of Germans and were holding them at Mogadishu, Somalia. Following these events, the taking of German hostages practically ended. When the United States gave Iran TOW anti-tank missiles in exchange for the release of hostages held in Lebanon, the hostage supply was quickly replenished by the taking of additional American citizens by the terrorist group.

THE CASE FOR DIFFERENT TACTICS FOR DIFFERENT SITUATIONS WITHIN A COHERENT STRATEGY

Israel's policy, stated by its late Prime Minister Yitzhak Rabin, has been a principled mixture of firmness and concessions. When hostages are held within Israel's borders, Israel responds with an armed rescue attempt and refuses to make concessions, even when the rescue attempt appears dangerous from the start. This firmness has been supported by the populace even when it has proved extremely costly in terms of the lives of children held by terrorists. When Israeli hostages are held in a hostile country where no armed assault by Israeli or friendly forces is possible, Israel will negotiate and make concessions in exchange for the lives of hostages. Extraordinary measures of security surrounding the flights of Israel's national airline, El Al, have made this rarely necessary. Finally, when Israeli hostages are held by terrorists in a country friendly to Israel, Israel's policy is to leave the handling of the matter to the friendly country.

This mixed strategy recognizes two critical factual variations. First, where hostages are held in a hostile country that will not permit rescue operations, a policy of firmness almost guarantees high costs to the hostages. Although a refusal to make concessions would tend to discourage future efforts to take hostages to that hostile country, the immediate price is extremely likely to include hostages' lives. And even if Israel does negotiate concessions in this situation, it does not compromise the clarity of Israel's announced policy of always preferring armed assault whenever possible.

Second, many of the short-term and long-term costs of making concessions may be diminished if the government whose citizens are held can disguise the fact that it is making concessions, perhaps by leaving the decision to the country where the hostages are being held or a third government that can satisfy the demands of the hostage takers. Even when its policy was firmest, the United States did not mind encouraging Israel to release very large numbers of prisoners to obtain the release of the passengers on TWA Flight 847 who were being held in Lebanon. Later, President Reagan believed that arranging the delivery of TOW missiles by Israel to Iran would eliminate the political costs of the United States making concessions to the Lebanese hostage-takers. He was plainly wrong. Other nations have agreed to early release—while public attention is directed elsewhere—of terrorists who have received long sentences. For example, Italy has allowed the escape of the terrorists imprisoned there for the hijacking of the *Achille Lauro*. The effect—disguising the fact that concessions are made—is the same.

In allowing a friendly country where Israeli hostages are held to decide whether to make concessions or attempt armed rescue, Israel accepts the different incentives of the "host" government. Its behavior may depend, Merari reminds us, on whether the government is the target of the terrorist demands and enmity. If it is not—as in the case of both Egypt and Italy when the *Achille Lauro* was seized—it may feel more free to make concessions without the risk of encouraging that particular group of hostage-takers to make future threats of concern to that government. A terrorist group's success may lead it to make additional threats against countries it regards as its enemy or against countries from whom it hopes to obtain concessions, but only international public-spiritedness makes these future threats relevant to the government of the place where the hostages are being held. Indeed, this is simply a special case of a more general category: whenever a government has reason to believe that concessions would not encourage future attacks on it, it has that much less reason to hold to a policy of firmness.

The United States has far greater diplomatic and military capacities to attempt rescue operations and to demand "no concessions" from a friendly government where American hostages are being held. There is thus less reason for the United States to qualify a "no concessions" policy with an exception for hostages held in a friendly country. The concessions the United States has made have largely been limited to American hostages in a hostile state, and even then only when the concessions could be disguised or hidden.

SOME SPECIAL CASES
For a country as powerful as the United States, with so much at stake in resisting terrorist threats and encouraging allies to resist those threats, there is a great deal to be said for a policy of refusing to make concessions, especially where an armed rescue attempt is possible but even where it is not (as with the hostages held in Lebanon at the time of the Iran-Contra scandal).[6] But it would be foolish to deny that there are trade-offs, particularly in a game that has two players.

CATASTROPHIC TERRORISM. Concessions would have to be made if there was no safe way of dealing with a terrorist's credible threat to harm tens of thousands of citizens, essentially holding, say, an entire city hostage. Such a threat would be highly unusual, but it must be taken seriously in light of the accessibility of chemical, biological, and nuclear weapons. Analytically, decision-makers must weigh the cost of an immense and credible threat against the cost of compliance with the demands made by the violent group. The cost of compliance includes whatever is given up to satisfy the demand plus the loss of national pride and prestige, and finally, the encouragement to future similar acts of terrorism.

The problem breaks into two parts: the threat and the reality. Anyone can threaten anything, including threatening nuclear devastation. No capacity to carry out such a threat is required to make it. To make concessions without knowing if the capacity or willingness are there would invite wholesale repetitions and the cost that would come with them. The United States needs (and has an Office of Threat Assessment whose job it is) to judge the credibility of threats. Governments must take some risks, requiring of terrorists some evidence of their ability to cause harm before taking threats seriously, or the cheapest of threats by terrorists can accomplish the most major of objectives.

If a threat appears to be real, however, and the risk is catastrophe, it may be necessary to make the concessions. But here the crucial problem is to make sure that the threat cannot be repeated by the same group again and again. The price of government concessions should include adequate steps to assure that the particular weapon or others like it will not continue to be available to the terrorists. In the long run, of course, any concessions should be followed by major steps to make sure that similar extortion cannot be carried out by other groups. These require knowing the mechanisms through which the instruments of catastrophic danger were obtained, transported, stored, and would be activated.

One other relationship is particularly important in the case of a catastrophic threat. If the capacity of the terrorist group to carry out the threat appears to depend upon the prior and continuing support or tolerance of a foreign nation, a threat by the United States to retaliate against that nation would be a form of legitimate self-defense and potentially effective. If a foreign nation was not responsible but could prevent the catastrophic consequences now or in the future, the United States would have to consider major military and economic pressure on that other nation, without regard to the technicalities of present interpretations of the international law of self-defense.

OTHER SITUATIONS OF GREAT DISPARITY BETWEEN THE COSTS AND BENEFITS OF CONCESSIONS. Much of the relationship between cost (long- and short-term) and benefits in terms of lives saved in the case of weapons of mass destruction is the same when there is simply an immense disparity between the size of the threat and the cost of compliance. For example, when the Unabomber threatened to continue to send package bombs to American academics and business managers unless his manifesto was published in the *Washington Post* and the *New York Times*, the United States wisely encouraged the publication. The concession was very small compared to the loss of even a single life. The risks of repetition by others would have to be far greater than they appeared to justify holding to the policy of firmness.

Moreover, there is no reason why the balance sheets of costs and benefits for the government and the terrorist group should be added up at an early date. That is, in appropriate circumstances the United States can announce that it will make concessions to avoid a threat, but that it will follow these concessions with a relentless and sophisticated effort to track down and punish the terrorists or otherwise to deny them the benefits of hostage-taking or some other form of threat. The intended effect of this strategy is to discourage future terrorism by the particular group or others without risking lives on this particular occasion.

There are two interesting variations of this straightforward strategy. First, the terrorists may well require a promise that there be no later retaliation by the United States. While it is of immense importance that the United States generally be thought reliable in keeping its promises and threats, a promise made under the threat of serious harm to American citizens might well be considered as non-binding as a promise made by an individual under coercion. This will naturally lead future terrorists to seek some greater assurance than a mere promise not to retaliate, but the advantage of creating exceptions to the reliability of the word of the government in this situation probably lies with the United States. Terrorists would want a regime of binding promises; their victims would not.

Second, the steps that follow concessions need not be limited to "punishment" of the terrorists. For example, if we are dealing with terrorists who are implacably hostile to our ally, Nation A, concessions to the terrorists can be followed by some new form of support to Nation A, perhaps military equipment. The total effect of the terrorists' strategy may then be to strengthen their enemy, an effect that is likely to discourage future terrorist attacks.

Conclusion

The immense audience attentive to a hostage situation or other sustained campaigns of terror is extremely attractive to terrorists, as is the demonstration of governmental impotence they frequently provide. Discouraging the tactic requires refusing concessions, but this is costly in the absence of an effective rescue capacity. For a diplomatic and military superpower, the case for developing that capacity on as broad a basis as possible and thereafter almost never making concessions is very strong. The United States has sometimes tried to disguise concessions as something else, but the effort generally fails.

Even for the United States, concessions may be sensible where the disparity between what is threatened and what is sought is immense. That will occur when the threat is catastrophic and also when the concession sought is trivial. In these cases concessions make sense, but then the United States should seek to keep the "account books" open and, after making concessions, find ways to assure that the tactic results in a net loss to the terrorists.

Chapter 4

International Cooperation in Preventing and Punishing Terrorism

When the targets of international terrorism are Americans, neither the state where the attack takes place nor any other state to which the terrorist may flee has nearly as great a motivation as the United States to catch and try the terrorists. For the United States to investigate in another country without the consent of its authorities is forbidden by international law and often by that country's law as well. Nor can the United States make an arrest within another country. What the terrorists have done abroad may not even violate U.S. statutes, which generally apply only within the United States.

The trial of a terrorist must bring four things together in one place: an applicable statutory prohibition, a willingness to prosecute, the necessary evidence, and the suspect. Terrorists can use the advantages of borders and easy transportation to assure that neither they (who may have fled to a safe location) nor the evidence (which may be outside the United States) are within the United States, the only jurisdiction with great enthusiasm for undertaking the risks of prosecuting acts by terrorists against American citizens.

The most straightforward solution to this problem of terrorists exploiting national sovereignty is for states to increase their cooperation, effectively pooling resources and coordinating efforts to prevent future terrorism and to catch and punish the perpetrators of past terrorist acts.

Cooperation in the field of prevention involves principally the exchange of information about dangerous groups and possible terrorist events. Such information is exchanged both among law enforcement agencies and among intelligence agencies of closely allied countries. When suicide bombers ravaged Israel in the spring of 1996, U.S. President Bill Clinton promised further exchanges with the intelligence agencies of Middle Eastern nations. But exchange requires trust that the information will not somehow be used against the provider or to reveal the provider's intelligence capacities or sources, and this requires a very special type of partner. Prevention can also involve planning meetings with the law enforcement agencies of friendly nations to discuss what would be done in the event of an act of catastrophic terrorism, or how several nations can together monitor signs of planning for an act of catastrophic terrorism such as the illegal sale of nuclear materials or the development of biological weapons, as in the case of the confrontation between the United Nations and Iraq in 1998.

These exchanges can be secret and, therefore, need not subject any nation to the threat of terrorist retaliation or political pressure from nations that support the terrorists' cause. However, because of such pressures, open cooperation in investigating, apprehending, prosecuting, and punishing terrorists is far less certain. So, let us begin with the possibilities of unilateral action by the United States to bring either evidence or the suspect from a foreign country to a trial in the United States. The limits of effective unilateral action provide the setting for then exploring the need, means, and difficulties of international cooperation.

The Limits of Unilateral Action

Conducting searches or making arrests in a foreign country without the consent of that country is in violation of international law and in violation of the law of that country. These activities are not, however, generally in violation of the law of the United States. This disparity creates a complicated context in which the primary consequences of unilateral action are diplomatic, not legal.

Since withdrawing its consent to the mandatory jurisdiction of the International Court of Justice in response to Sandinista allegations of illegal U.S. attacks on Nicaragua, the United States can no longer be brought before any international tribunal without its consent. Other nations may refuse to honor treaties requiring cooperation with the United States if the U.S. action would violate international law, but that has no immediate consequence when cooperation is not needed because we can unilaterally find or bring the evidence and the defendant within the United States.

The most serious impact of a violation of international law is at the diplomatic level. Long-time friends, like Mexico (or like Egypt and Italy in the case of the *Achille Lauro*) will do everything in their power to insist that a superpower ally remain within the bounds of international law and recognize their sovereignty. After the abduction of a Mexican citizen, described shortly, Mexico's protests were powerful and influential. Much of Latin America joined in Mexico's vocal outrage. The international standing of Mexico, Egypt, and Italy, or of Algeria and Syria in the case of TWA Flight 847—and the importance of good relations with these states to the United States— makes our compliance with international law far more important.

The diplomatic problems are far less severe if the actions are taken in a state with which our relations are very bad. But there, the danger to U.S. agents would be grave. For example, when the United States went after General Manuel Noriega, it paid a heavy price in lives and property damage to effect the seizure.[1] Independent action in Beirut in response to the hijacking of TWA Flight 847 would have been equally dangerous.

Compliance with U.S. law—as contrasted with international law—is obviously mandatory and of immense political importance to any U.S. administration. A failure to respect U.S. law is grounds for impeachment of the president. Moreover, customary international law is generally, for many purposes, considered part of U.S. law. But customary international law, of the sort that prohibits searches and arrests in a foreign country, can be overruled by Congress and can be set aside by the president. So, with high enough executive authority, the unilateral actions we are discussing are not made violations of U.S. law by the mere fact that they violate traditional international obligations. Indeed, in the aftermath of the terrorist attacks in the mid-1980s, the Reagan and the Bush administrations clarified that arrests abroad engineered or executed by U.S. agents and other duly authorized law enforcement efforts in violation of another nation's sovereignty did not violate U.S. statutes.

Executive orders signed by the president forbid assassination by any U.S. agency. Thus, U.S. agencies cannot engage in secret intelligence operations of the sort that Israel's intelligence service Mossad apparently used to execute several members of the Black September terrorist group that had murdered Israeli athletes in Munich, Germany in 1972. British military agents killed three members of the Irish Republican Army in an incident at Gibraltar that British authorities have never adequately explained. (See Chapter 7.) If these killings were intentional that, too, would be forbidden to U.S. personnel. But apart from this fundamental prohibition, there are few other restrictions in U.S. statutes or executive rules that bar unilateral law enforcement action abroad by U.S. agents. An opinion of the Department of Justice's Office of Legal Counsel written for Attorney General Richard Thornburg found such actions to be within the statutory jurisdiction of the FBI, although it recommended that each should be specifically authorized at a very high level.

Finally, two U.S. Supreme Court cases established that there is no constitutional bar to searches or arrests by U.S. agents abroad. On February 7, 1985, drug enforcement agent Enrique Camarena-Salazar was kidnapped near the U.S. Consulate in Guadalajara, Jalisco, Mexico. One month later, his mutilated body was discovered about sixty miles outside of Guadalajara. The efforts of the Drug Enforcement Administration (DEA) to find out who was responsible, to gather the necessary evidence for trial in the United States, and to bring the suspects back to the United States led to both cases.

Rene Verdugo Urquidez, a chief lieutenant of a Mexican drug czar, was arrested by Mexican authorities in 1986. He was blindfolded, handcuffed, and driven to the U.S./Mexican border by individuals, including officials, acting at the request of the DEA. There he was handed over to U.S. marshals who had a warrant for his arrest. DEA agents working with Mexican law enforcement officials searched his home in Mexicali, Mexico, seizing evidence that helped convict

Verdugo Urquidez of Camarena-Salazar's murder. Dr. Humberto Alvarez Machain, who was accused of injecting Camarena-Salazar with drugs in order to keep him awake while being tortured, was seized by Mexican police at his office in Guadalajara, Mexico. The police had been hired by DEA agents to find Alvarez Machain, kidnap him, and fly him to El Paso, Texas where he was placed under arrest by DEA agents.

Mexico had refused to extradite both Verdugo Urquidez and Alvarez Machain, relying on its general policy of refusing to extradite its own citizens; but there was also suspicion of the involvement of high-level Mexican officials in the kidnapping and murder.

In *Verdugo-Urquidez*, the U.S. Supreme Court concluded that the Fourth Amendment to the United States Constitution did not protect aliens with no substantial tie to the United States from searches conducted without Fourth Amendment protections abroad by, or with the cooperation of, the U.S. law enforcement agents.[2] In *Alvarez-Machain*, the Supreme Court upheld the legality of the defendant's trial in the United States, even if he had been abducted illegally under Mexican and customary international law.[3] The situation might have been different if our extradition treaty with Mexico had prohibited the abduction, but the court would not read that understanding— now eagerly sought by Mexico and other Latin American countries— into the indefinite words of the treaty.

It is thus not the mandate of U.S. law but the powerful demands of maintaining good relations with other countries that prevent the U.S. from engaging in most unilateral actions to bring home the evidence or the suspect after a terrorist attack on the United States abroad. Occasionally, it may be possible to act unilaterally abroad without serious foreign policy implications. The FBI, for example, succeeded in luring Fawaz Younis, one of those involved in the hijacking of TWA Flight 847, onto international waters in the fall of 1987. Law enforcement officials seized him there and brought him back to the United States where he was convicted after trial. But this is a tactic that cannot be frequently repeated, so international cooperation is generally essential.

The Formal Instruments of International Cooperation

It is important to distinguish between the formal mechanisms of law enforcement cooperation—extradition and mutual legal assistance treaties—and the political conditions of cooperation that apply even among nations that are close allies. I begin with the legal forms of cooperation.

When U.S. citizens, property, or facilities have been attacked in a foreign country, the U.S. objective is to bring the evidence and the perpetrators into an American court for trial under a criminal statute that applies to terrorist acts outside of our borders.

Friendly nations will only cooperate in providing evidence or extraditing the suspect if the U.S. statute under which the suspect will be tried reaches no further in its extraterritorial application than international law allows. The United States could not, for example, successfully demand extradition of a French citizen who killed an Austrian, or even an American, in a barroom brawl in Paris. International law does not recognize such a broad claim of national power to control or punish events abroad.

Under customary international law, the United States may apply its criminal laws to events that took place abroad, even if they do not have any intended effects within our borders, if: (1) the statute applies to crimes by our own nationals; (2) the "protective principle" is involved because the acts threaten the integrity or security of the United States itself; or (3) the suspect has committed a "universal" crime—one so threatening to international order as to be widely considered appropriate for trial anywhere. In most cases of political violence specifically targeted against American citizens or American interests because they are American, either the protective principle or the notion of universal offenses will apply. Indeed, there are several international agreements—the Montreal, Hague, Tokyo, and Hostage Conventions—which provide that every signatory nation, of which the United States is one, shall have jurisdiction over specified terrorist offenses.[4]

Taking advantage of this authorization under international law, the United States has passed a number of statutes with extraterritorial reach. The applicable statute in the Younis case was the Aircraft Sabotage Act of 1984, which applies to anyone who "destroys a civil aircraft registered in a country other than the United States."[5] The Hostage-Taking Act of 1984 also rests on a notion of universal crime and allows trial whenever "the offender is found in the United States." (One can be "found in the United States" after being seized abroad and brought into the United States for trial.) Still other statutes apply to terrorist assaults on Americans abroad.[6]

Against the background of such U.S. statutes, which are firmly grounded in international law notions of acceptable "legislative" jurisdiction, the United States has a basis for asking friendly governments for cooperation—formal under treaties of extradition, and informal in seeking permission and assistance for U.S. investigations abroad. (Allowing the FBI to investigate within another nation's borders is far more useful than simply getting whatever assistance foreign police agencies may offer out of comity, for only the U.S. investigators are likely to be highly motivated by an attack on U.S. citizens abroad.) The CIA may also be able to obtain information, often from its foreign counterparts, although the terms on which it obtains the information may make it unavailable to, or unusable by, law enforcement.

These informal methods of cooperation in obtaining information and evidence can be bolstered by formal treaties. A mutual legal assistance treaty requires the treaty partner to take, upon U.S. request, investigative steps within the scope of the treaty, and to take these steps in ways that render the product admissible in U.S. courts. An extradition treaty requires the treaty partner either to turn over to the United States, or to try under its own law, an individual whom the United States has probable cause to believe violated U.S. law.

A number of prerequisites must be satisfied before either type of treaty obligation can be asserted. First, the United States must have an internationally recognized basis for concerning itself with actions that took place abroad. Second, for extradition (although not generally for legal assistance), the conduct must be criminal in both countries and not previously punished abroad. Third, many countries, although not the United States, will refuse a request to extradite one of its nationals on the ground that sending its own citizen to another country for trial is a violation of fundamental rights. Fourth, almost all such treaties have a broad exception for what the requested country may consider to be a "political" offense and many have an exception where there is doubt as to whether the individual can obtain a fair trial in the requesting state. For example, members of the European Union will not extradite an individual who may be subjected to the death penalty in the United States, until the United States has agreed that the death penalty will not be sought.

These requirements create substantial leeway for a state to refuse to assist its treaty partner. It can decide to try the suspect itself, proceeding sometimes with less than great enthusiasm in the hopes of acquittal or in the expectation of arranging an early release after a short sentence. It can find technical objections to the request for extradition, as Italy did in the case of the U.S. request for the extradition of Abu Abbas in the *Achille Lauro* case. It can apply the political offense exception. It can try the individual for another offense, delaying any response until he or she has been convicted and served a prison term. The availability of such escapes means that the treaty vehicles for cooperation depend greatly upon diplomacy and politics.

The Politics of Cooperation

Chapter 3 described how, on June 14, 1985, Arab terrorists hijacked TWA Flight 847 en route to Rome from Athens and forced the crew to fly to Beirut, where they killed an American Navy diver, Robert Stetham, and for seventeen days held hostage 39 passengers, mainly Americans, and the crew. Eighteen months later, Germany arrested one of the accused hijackers, Mohammed Hammadei, a 22-year-old Lebanese, as he departed from a plane in Frankfurt, Germany, carrying a suitcase full of explosives. Someone had provided essential intelligence to the Germans.

The United States immediately sought Hammadei's extradition under its treaty with Germany. The plane was American, there were numerous American passengers, there was an American homicide victim, and the hijackers had made a careful effort to single out and terrorize American passengers. These facts, and the absence of German interests and contacts, made the case close to perfect for extradition. In addition, the U.S. Aircraft Sabotage Act and Hostage-Taking Act gave U.S. authorities extraterritorial jurisdiction in cases of hostage-taking, hijacking, and aircraft sabotage—a claim of jurisdiction that would be recognized by Germany because of international conventions.

International treaties and informal understandings among long-term allies who are linked by close economic and political ties can provide a powerful force in international relations. However, treaties of extradition and mutual assistance in obtaining evidence are regularly written with room for political judgment about their applicability. The procedures for compliance generally require not only action by the courts of the "requested" state, Germany in Hammadei's case, but also approval by that state's political authorities.

Under the treaty, Germany had several alternatives for handling Hammadei. First, it could have extradited him to the United States, assuming the United States had filed a proper request. Second, Germany could have tried him in a German court for violation of German statutes. If Hammadei's acts were universal crimes, any state could try Hammadei under international law so long as the acts were forbidden by the state's domestic law as well. Third, Germany could have initially tried Hammadei only for attempting to import explosives and other arms, thus delaying the questions of extradition and trial for hijacking, hostage-taking, and murder. Germany then could have waited for the expiration of Hammadei's sentence for these crimes before facing the other issues. As a practical matter, Germany might have released Hammadei on the grounds that the treaty didn't require his extradition, as Italy had done with Abu Abbas in the *Achille Lauro* case, although this might violate the treaty.

The extradition treaty left Germany free to choose among the first three alternatives. When the suspect is in the requested state's custody, extradition treaties generally offer the requested state the choice of trial or extradition and the choice as to the sequence of trials if it can bring more than one charge. While many international law scholars might argue that a preferable system would be to extradite when the requesting state has far better reasons for trying the suspect than the requested state, international law does not require this.

Germany could also have relied on the "political offense" exception to extradition obligations. Found in almost every treaty, the exception allows the judicial and political authorities of the requested state to refuse extradition on the ground that the crime itself was "political." The political offense exception to the obligation to extradite or try can have a devastating impact on the few international conventions outlawing airplane hijacking, attacks on diplomats and other "internationally protected persons," and hostage-taking. None of these international conventions provides for effective sanctions against states that ignore their obligations, and states can interpret the "political offense" exception very broadly.

Even when close allies are involved, as in the case of the United States and Great Britain, Israel, Germany, France, or Italy, there is no agreement on what constitutes a political offense. Some would include any crime committed for political reasons. The United States has departed substantially from its early nineteenth-century tradition of identifying with revolutionary causes and thus rejects such a broad exception. Today, the United States would eliminate the political offense exception for ordinary violent crimes, at least when soldiers or other security forces are not the targets of the crimes. The British-American Supplementary Extradition Treaty of 1985 adopts this general direction.

Within a week of Hammadei's arrest, two German nationals were taken hostage in Beirut. The kidnappers demanded that Germany not extradite Hammadei to the United States but instead release him in exchange for the two Germans. Because Germany had several legally valid options for handling Hammadei, political considerations would largely determine Germany's choice.

Fearing that the routine procedure for dealing with extradition requests might lead either to the execution of the hostages or to the disruption of U.S.-German relations, Chancellor Kohl set up a special working group, which never sent the United States' extradition request through normal channels to the courts of Hesse, the German state where Hammadei was arrested. The decisions were to be made in Bonn whether to extradite Hammadei, to charge him in Germany for the hijacking under the "universal" jurisdiction of all states in matters of piracy and hijacking, to try Hammadei initially only for the passport and explosives charges, or to release him. Considerations of Atlantic and Middle East foreign policy, concern for the lives of the hostages, a desire to have German investigators discover the reasons for the importation of the explosives, and other policy matters would determine Germany's decision, often competing with the moral force of its treaty with the United States. Chancellor Kohl decided to try Hammadei for the hijacking and murder charges in Germany. He was duly convicted.

Trying terrorists in domestic courts can reduce diplomatic pressures from the victimized state, but pressure from terrorists will not disappear so long as the terrorist remains in danger of severe punishment. The pressures and dangers are eliminated only if the political authorities of a reluctant requested state can reassure the terrorist group that the suspects will not receive severe sentences. This requires using government influence with local prosecutors, and perhaps even wielding some influence over the courts. Then the state will be able to avoid extradition by promising the requesting state that there will be a trial and still avoid the wrath of the terrorists. In this way, it may try to protect its citizens held hostage and further foreign policy interests with national allies of the terrorists without alienating a powerful ally that was the victim of terrorism.[7]

France chose this solution in the 1986 case of Georges Ibrahim Abdallah. Abdallah led a small terrorist group called the Lebanese Armed Revolutionary Factions (FARL). The group primarily targeted diplomatic officials. In 1981, a gunman shot and wounded First Counselor Christian Chapman of the American Embassy in Paris. On January 18, 1982, the deputy military attaché, Lieutenant Colonel Charles Ray, was killed, and FARL publicly assumed responsibility for the murder. Three months later, a terrorist used a Czech-made 7.65 caliber pistol to kill Yacov Barsimantov, the second secretary of the Israeli Embassy in Paris. In late 1982, FARL targeted the U.S. commercial attaché and the Israeli Embassy in Paris. During 1984,

FARL claimed responsibility for the assassination in Rome of General Leamon Hunt, American chief of the international observation force in the Sinai, and for the wounding of Robert Homme, American representative to the European Parliament in Strasbourg. Abdallah was also suspected in the 1976 assassination of Francis Meloy, the American ambassador in Beirut.

Abdallah was arrested in France in the fall of 1984 and charged with relatively minor crimes. Some months later, Gilles Sydney Peyrolles, the director of the French cultural center in Tripoli, Libya, was kidnapped in Lebanon, and the French government was told that the kidnappers would release Peyrolles only in exchange for Abdallah. An activist from President Mitterrand's Socialist Party who had close ties with Algeria's ruling party arranged for an Algerian lieutenant to visit with Abdallah in Paris. Abdallah gave the Algerian the names of the people to whom he should speak. The Algerian then met with FARL representatives in Beirut.

Before there was hard evidence linking Abdallah with the shootings of Chapman, Ray, and Barsimantov, the French foreign minister obtained the release of Peyrolles by indicating to the FARL kidnappers that Abdallah would be released after a very short sentence for relatively minor crimes. After the discovery of important new evidence of murder and in response to the initiation of new and more serious proceedings against Abdallah, FARL launched a series of bombings throughout Paris, and Algeria complained that it had been betrayed by France.

The French security minister met with the judge in charge of investigating the more serious charges against Abdallah and urged him to delay his decision. An official in the Justice Ministry ordered the public prosecutor's office to dismiss the charges against Abdallah, a directive the prosecutor disobeyed, but after Abdallah's conviction, the French prosecutor urged the sentencing court to impose a sentence of no more than ten years, referring to the risk to the French hostages.

The United States had hired a lawyer under the provisions of French criminal procedure, which allow victims to play a part in the trial of criminal cases, seeking damages at the end of the trial. The distinguished French lawyer for the United States and for the widow of Lieutenant Colonel Charles Ray made an impassioned appeal that the judges should put the danger of reprisals out of their mind. The government could pardon Abdallah if that was its political judgement, but as to the court: "It is not for you to do the state's work the first time a major terrorist appears before a French court . . . . your only mission is to deliver justice, not services. The only state for you should be the state of law."[8] The judges sentenced Abdallah to life imprisonment. Nonetheless, the case highlights the possibility of limiting and controlling a prosecution that itself is used to avoid extradition.

Dealing with Unfriendly States Providing Sanctuary for Terrorists

Germany and France are allies tied to the United States by an elaborate network of collaboration. Because of these ties, both Hammadei and Abdallah were tried, although neither was extradited. But what if the terrorist escapes to a state that has no such bonds to the United States and, consequently, has no extradition or mutual legal assistance treaty with the United States?

How can a state that has been victimized by political violence elicit cooperation from a state used as a sanctuary by, or providing assistance to, the violent group? It can use its own political resources or turn to its allies for help. What is required depends upon the sanctuary state's attitude toward the violent group. If a sanctuary state tolerates terrorist activities in its territory because it is unwilling to antagonize the terrorist group, strong responses are available to the victim state. The United States may discourage travel to a particular nation, reduce the size of an embassy, or vote against particular loans. If Greece refused to extradite the terrorist Mohamed Rashid, who detonated a bomb on an American jet flying over Hawaii in 1982, the United States could, for example, oppose in the name of safety Greece's bid to host the one-hundredth anniversary of the modern Olympics.[9] If the United States is dealing with a sanctuary state that actively supports terrorism, it could break all economic and diplomatic relations or, more dramatically, respond militarily, invoking the doctrine of self-defense, as the United States did in bombing Libya in April 1986 in retaliation for the Libyan role in the bombing of a disco frequented by U.S. military personnel in Berlin.

The victim state's capacity to use some types of sanctions, particularly economic and diplomatic measures, to persuade a sanctuary state to take action against a terrorist group generally depends upon the victim state's ability to rally influential allies. Without a broad base of support for the victim state from allied nations, a sanctuary state will simply make up elsewhere for economic or other measures taken against it by the victim state.

The "G-8" nations—the group of seven largest industrialized nations, plus Russia—share a common concern about terrorism, so they may cooperate to effectively pressure any state providing sanctuary to terrorists. Acting together, these economic giants can bring very powerful economic threats or diplomatic measures against any sanctuary state that supports political violence. For example, the United States and the six other nations that, before the addition of Russia, constituted the "Group of Seven" (G-7) effectively threatened South Africa with the cancellation of air traffic because of a failure to punish terrorists.

Regrettably, numerous factors limit the capacity of the G-8 nations to act in concert against terrorism. Each of the eight has different foreign policy commitments and ties. France, Italy, and to some extent Russia, have historic, economic, and demographic ties to Syria and Libya to a degree that the United States, Great Britain, Germany, Canada, and Japan do not always share. In addition, each country confronts different domestic political pressures when dealing with terrorism. For example, with a large and passionate Irish-American population, the United States has often been slow to extradite IRA terrorists. Germany must deal carefully with even violent political dissent in light of its history of Nazi oppression of political opponents. Each of the eight is subject to different dangers of retaliation from a politically violent group or its state sponsors depending on physical proximity, ease of travel, and the nationality of any hostage being held.

The United States cannot readily use the economic and diplomatic leverage of being the world's only superpower to overcome
these differences with its closest allies about how to deal with threats
of political violence. In the Antiterrorism Act of 1996, the Congress
forbade various forms of assistance to countries that provide assistance to a state supporting terrorism, but these provisions would not
generally apply to our major allies. The act also prohibits the sale of
defense articles or services to any "foreign country that the President
determines . . . is not cooperating fully with United States antiterrorism efforts."[10] Still, as was shown in 1997 by France's defiance of a
U.S. ban on certain transactions with Iran, the United States has too
many beneficial relationships with its closest allies and cannot risk
rupturing them over the issue of cooperating in using sanctions
against particular nations offering sanctuary to particular terrorist
groups. The most the United States can generally do is encourage the
other G-8 states to work together in dealing with a common threat of
political violence in order to increase the capacity of each to put
pressure on states that would otherwise support political violence or
remain neutral.

Informal Cooperation

Given the difficulties of formal cooperation by such means as extradition for bringing terrorists to trial, it is not surprising that nations
have developed informal alternatives that do not require the same
measure of state-to-state cooperation. In particular, the United States
has developed the forms of police-to-police cooperation more than
any other country. As Ethan Nadelmann explains in *Cops Across
Borders*: "The common sentiment that a cop is a cop no matter whose
badge he or she wears, and that a criminal is a criminal no matter
what his or her citizenship is or where the crime was committed,
serves as a kind of transgovernmental value system overriding
political conflicts between governments."[11]

FBI Director Louis J. Freeh has stated that the FBI liaison offices
abroad, which will number 46 by 1998, and their ability to deal
directly with foreign police agencies in requesting and providing

native assistance, are the most significant factor in the Bureau's ability to deal with international crimes against the United States or its citizens. The FBI presence abroad is still small compared to the presence of the DEA, which has its own police-to-police contacts. Informal cooperation among intelligence agencies also plays a role. For example, both the DEA and the CIA played significant roles in tracking and helping to capture Ramzi Yousef, the convicted mastermind behind the World Trade Center bombing and the leader of a plot to bomb eleven U.S. airliners simultaneously as they flew over the Pacific.

Police in the Philippines, watching for an attack during a 1995 visit of the Pope, first uncovered the airliner plot when a bomb-making factory caught fire. Discovering that the plot might involve terrorist attacks on U.S. airliners, the Philippine police promptly informed their American counterparts in the U.S. embassy. They also provided a fingerprint found on the premises that the FBI matched with the World Trade Center fugitive Yousef. Yousef fled, but the FBI, with the agreement of foreign counterparts, followed leads to Pakistan, where Yousef was captured after an informant walked into the American Embassy, motivated by a $2 million reward offered by the United States, and turned Yousef in.

While police-to-police cooperation may be extremely useful in a particular case, U.S. law enforcement efforts abroad are illegal under local and international law and are impracticable without at least the tacit cooperation of the host government. The host government need not take any significant action itself or openly assume responsibility for a terrorist's arrest and transfer to U.S. control. But it must implicitly, if not explicitly, consent to the U.S. role.

Pakistan's acquiescence in U.S. efforts in the Yousef case was brought about by high-level diplomacy. At the time of the Yousef case, Pakistan was in jeopardy of being added to the U.S. State Department's official list of countries that sponsor international terrorism, which would have subjected it to trade restrictions and foreign aid penalties. Its position was particularly sensitive because Yousef had entered the United States on Pakistan International Airlines without a U.S. visa, a requirement foreign carriers are supposed to check before allowing passengers to board U.S.-bound flights. Moreover, a scheduled exchange of visits between Hillary Rodham Clinton and Prime Minister Benazir Bhutto could have been threatened. Similarly, the Philippines had its own political reasons for cooperating, as it learned that Yousef was also plotting to kill the Pope on his visit to the Philippines.

Very similar cooperation led to the arrest of Abdul Hakim Murad, an alleged co-conspirator in Yousef's plan for airliner bombings and the assassination of the Pope. Finally, in perhaps the most spectacular example of informal cooperation involving American authorities abroad, five FBI agents disguised in native garb arrested Mir Aimal Kansi in central Pakistan in June 1997, and quickly returned him to the United States where he was convicted of opening fire on CIA employees outside the main gates to the agency's Langley, Virginia, headquarters, killing two.

Conclusion

The fact that there are many more instances of international terrorism against the United States than domestic terrorism in part reflects the advantages for terrorists of putting themselves beyond the area in which U.S. law enforcement officers can conduct investigations and develop information and evidence consistently with international law. The effect of international law prohibiting search or arrest abroad does not flow from a threat of enforcement either in U.S. courts or in the International Court of Justice. Rather, international law has major force diplomatically. Allies and friendly nations will resist any effort by foreign law enforcement officials to seize their citizens and transport them thousands of miles to a foreign country.

The United States therefore must rely on international cooperation under bilateral treaties to offset the advantage that terrorists attacking U.S. citizens and interests can obtain by separating themselves from U.S. jurisdiction. Long before any crisis, the United States can increase its ability to prosecute terrorists by laying the legal groundwork for effective international law enforcement. But our allies retain the capacity to protect national interests that are inconsistent with cooperation with the United States on a particular occasion by invoking a variety of loopholes and forms of discretion built into extradition and mutual legal assistance treaties. Diplomacy and foreign policy can reduce the tendency to invoke such escape hatches, as can intelligent efforts to monitor and even take part in foreign trials.

Chapter 5

State-Sponsored Terrorism and Retaliation

All the ambiguities and dilemmas of responding to state-sponsored terrorism were present in the spring of 1996 in Israel. Retaliating for Katyusha rocket attacks on northern Israel by Hezbollah guerrillas but, symbolically, also for suicide bombers sent by a different terrorist group (Hamas) to kill dozens of Israelis, Israel launched major air, sea, and artillery attacks on Lebanon. The aim was to force Syria, the dominant power in Lebanon, to restrain the guerrillas of Hezbollah and, many thought, to bolster the lagging spirits of Israelis during an election campaign when the government of Prime Minister Shimon Peres was being accused of being soft.

A tragic mistake in targeting killed one hundred Lebanese huddling on a UN base, many of them women and children. Added to the other death, dislocation, and terror, the effect was to solidify support among Lebanese civilians for Hezbollah and to create outrage among Israel's allies, undermining the credibility of any Israeli threat of continuing bombardment. Striking directly at Syria would have risked war and could only have been justified by a demonstration of continuing Syrian responsibility for the actions of Hezbollah guerillas in Lebanon. But striking indirectly at Syria had weakened Israel's position as much as Syria's.

Plainly, retaliation is a morally and politically complicated matter, risking the lives of innocent people to make a point with their leaders and, in doing so, generating powerful opposition as well as fear. These risks are equally present when the United States uses

military force to respond to state-supported or tolerated terrorism—
for example, when President Reagan ordered the bombing of Libya
in 1986 and President Clinton used cruise missiles against Iraq in
1993. Still, in the world of military force, it is very different being a
superpower and very dangerous being a state sponsoring terrorism
against a superpower. In this chapter, we will consider why states
sponsor terrorism despite the risks of a military response by the
target of the terrorists and how effective such responses are.

War by Proxy or Secret Agents

For centuries, nations have seen the advantages of encouraging and
supporting violence by those rebelling against their enemies. French
support for the American war of independence from Britain is an
important example. Two centuries later, the United States has provided open and public support for one side in a civil war, although
that side may itself have engaged in secret violence against civilian
targets as part of wider, more open warfare, so long as the violence
is kept at home, and does not become a form of international terrorism. Examples would include our support for rebel forces in Angola,
Nicaragua, Cambodia, and Afghanistan after its seizure by the Soviet
Union. Such support has many of the same advantages as having
another state as an ally against your enemy.

Supporting a terrorist group has similar advantages to supporting a rebellious army or a foreign nation at war with an enemy, but
it has one more as well: if the sponsorship can be hidden, the violence
against one's enemy can be safe and unaccountable. The nation that
is the target of the terrorism cannot respond, as it might to a direct
attack, unless and until it can develop evidence of its enemy's
responsibility. Nor can the domestic opposition object to violent
adventures for which its government disclaims responsibility. For
example, the Reagan administration at times disclaimed responsibility for its support of the activities of the "Contras" while secretly
supporting them with weapons to fight the Sandinista revolutionary
government in Nicaragua during the 1980s. For much of this period
Congress had forbidden any form of support for the military activi-

ties of the Contras. For both these reasons, the relatively minor disadvantage of keeping a nation's support secret—the inability to negotiate directly with one's enemies and demand concessions in exchange for a reduction in violence—is often offset by the benefits.

A nation's support of somewhat independent groups engaged in terrorist activities against the nation's opponents can vary in ways that bear importantly on its responsibility. At one extreme, the "supporting" nation may be unable to control the activities of powerful groups within its borders. This has often been true of Lebanon, which could not deny operational freedom to well-armed Hezbollah forces. At the opposite extreme, a nation may freely make available its territory, resources such as weapons and money, its ability to transport people and goods across boundaries under diplomatic cover, such facilities as travel documents and safe houses, and even ultimately sanctuary. Syria seems to have done almost all of this for terrorists who attempted in 1986 to blow up an El Al aircraft leaving Britain for Israel. Between the extremes, a state may be disapproving but unwilling to bear the costs of stopping or pursuing terrorists (as Egypt may have been in the case of the *Achille Lauro*); it may be willing to tolerate, but not support, their activities; or it may provide some limited support. There is no clear international understanding of where along this continuum a state becomes so responsible as to be subject under international law and practice to sanctions or military response.

Whatever its level of responsibility, a state providing some form of tolerance or support for terrorist groups will try to hide the evidence of its role. The result is that, inescapably, the problems of proof for the nation victimized by the violent group are severe. Nor is there any international agreement as to what level of proof is necessary for a response. Indeed, in light of the realities of foreign relations, a nation is likely to demand a higher level of proof of complicity before acting against some nations than against others.

The U.S. Department of State, for example, is responsible for identifying states that have repeatedly provided support for international terrorism. Iraq, a long-time supporter of some of the most violent terrorist groups, was removed from the list from 1982 to 1990 (when it invaded Kuwait). That decision was plainly influenced by the position of the United States with regard to the war between Iraq and Iran. The State Department has also been careful to insist on strong evidence before it adds a state to its list. In 1991, the only six countries listed were Cuba, Iran, Iraq, Libya, North Korea, and Syria. The State Department did not have on its list Eastern European countries whose major support for international terrorism only became unmistakable after the collapse of their Communist regimes.

Striking Back

The reasons students of criminal law have given for punishment provide a handy checklist of the reasons why states might strike back at another state that is sponsoring terrorist attacks. There are three forward-looking, preventative reasons. The strike might incapacitate some of the people or some part of the arsenal of the terrorist group. It might, alternatively, accomplish "specific" deterrence by vividly reminding the sponsoring state of the costs of its support of terrorism. Retaliation might even, more generally, send a message of "general deterrence" to all states that might be tempted by the advantages of sponsoring terrorist attacks for which they hope they cannot be held accountable.

The Israeli response to Hezbollah rocket attacks on northern Israel in the spring of 1996 is a reminder that other, less preventative purposes may also be at work. Retribution for a wrong done is a powerful motivator for nations, as it is for individuals. Moreover, just as punishment of criminals sometimes seems necessary to maintain the morale of law-abiding citizens, punishment of a state that has secretly inflicted harm on another state's citizens may be crucial to prevent a demoralizing feeling of helplessness, such as affected Israel after the set of suicide bombings organized by Hamas. Finally, the state targeted by another state's terrorist allies may find it important to signal to its own friends that it is far from powerless, that it is not as vulnerable as it has been made to seem. That was certainly one of the major motivations for the dramatic action of U.S. authorities in response to the hijacking of the *Achille Lauro*.

Such purposes as incapacitating, deterring, or "getting even" need not involve military action; the alternative is economic and diplomatic sanctions. But generally these require substantial international cooperation. Even the United States may not constitute a massive enough market in the modern world to impose meaningful economic sanctions by itself, although that was precisely what it attempted to do with regard to economic sanctions on Libya in early 1986.[1] For other nations, and generally for the United States as well, economic and diplomatic sanctions are only powerful enough if they are implemented in concert by substantially all the nations on whose trade, assistance, investments, and travel the punished country depends. It has proved difficult to bring about this cooperation. Their differing foreign policies and vulnerabilities to countermeasures by terrorists have prevented the great Western powers, including Japan, from uniting on economic sanctions. Only the United States and Britain have often been willing to impose significant economic sanctions, or prohibitions on airplane flights, or significant diplomatic sanctions on such identified sponsors of international terrorism as Libya, Iran, and Syria. The same difficulties have generally prevented the imposition of sanctions by United Nations Security Council resolution. The first time this occurred in response to terrorism was in 1992, when the Security Council imposed economic and diplomatic sanctions against Libya for its failure to turn over the people apparently responsible for the bombing of Pan Am Flight 103 over Lockerbie, Scotland.

A military response is more readily available, at least for the world's only superpower. The United States responded with massive bombing from the air to the Libyan terrorist bombing of a nightclub in Berlin in 1986 and again, some years later, the United States launched cruise missiles in response to an Iraqi effort in April 1993 to assassinate former President George Bush.

Only one of the purposes of punishment described above, specific deterrence, constitutes a justification under international law for military retaliation against a state that sponsors terrorism. Article 2(4) of the United Nations Charter states that: "All members shall refrain in their international relations from the threat or use of force against the territorial integrity or political independence of any state." However, the breadth of this prohibition is limited by Article 51, which states: "Nothing in the present Charter shall impair the inherent right of individual or collective self-defense if an armed attack occurs against a member of the United Nations, until the Security Council has taken measures necessary to maintain international peace and security."

Thus, a military reprisal, which is certainly "the use of force against the territorial integrity or political independence of any state," must be justified in terms of "individual . . . self-defense." It must be intended to end a course of continuing conduct threatening to the nation relying on the doctrine of self-defense. It cannot simply be intended to "get even" or to serve one of the other purposes, except for specific deterrence to defend the threatened nation against continued or additional terrorist attacks.

Even in this context, there is substantial debate as to whether self-defense can be used to justify a response to anything other than an armed incursion by identified troops into the defender's territory. Some argue that only such incursions are clear enough acts to justify self-help: that in all other cases there is too likely to be a mistake about who is responsible for terrorism and too little urgency about resolving that matter to justify a form of military retaliation that may lead to escalation and war. Still, denying that sponsoring terrorism is a form of aggression against which a country may defend itself would leave the targets defenseless until and unless the Security Council acted.

It is difficult to define and prove the level of sponsorship of terrorist acts that would warrant retaliation in self-defense. Presumably, a state that was helpless to prevent its territory being used could not be attacked; nor might mere tolerance of the presence of a terrorist group be adequate to justify armed retaliation. No one knows, however, how much more should be necessary before retaliation is justified. The responses of U.S. administrations suggest that the United States would hold a country responsible for a terrorist act only if sufficient proof existed that the country's own agents were assisting the attack. This was certainly the standard employed by

President Clinton in 1993 against Iraq. Independent attacks by sub-state groups have not been included in this category, even when the groups in question were dependent on states for their existence and operations and even when their attacks were undoubtedly designed to serve the host country's interests.

It is also unclear how sure the retaliating state must be of its case or whether it has any obligation to set forth its evidence or to give the state it accuses of sponsoring terrorism an opportunity to respond diplomatically. As to the first of these issues, President Clinton quietly took a substantial step toward a more responsible procedure in 1993 when he asked the Justice Department to give him its own conclusion—to compare with those of his intelligence agencies—on the clarity of Iraqi responsibility for an attempt to assassinate President Bush in Kuwait. Using different methods and evidence and applying different standards of proof, the Department of Justice reached the same conclusion as the intelligence agencies, and the likelihood of error was greatly reduced.

Acceptance of the need to justify any military reprisal against a state-sponsor of terrorism in terms of international law has one serious drawback. From the point of view of both domestic public opinion and international politics, any military retaliatory action must be launched relatively soon after the act of terrorism that triggered it. As the investigation of the mid-air bombing of Pan Am Flight 103 shows, a long time may pass before sufficiently clear proof is obtained concerning the identity of the perpetrators. The delay associated with applying highly protective criteria for accountability for terrorism may often exclude military reprisal as a countermeasure, although the passage of several months did not preclude the retaliatory strike against Iraq in 1993.

These are significant problems, for state sponsors of terrorism often do their best to conceal their involvement for the very purpose of avoiding international condemnation and potential retaliation by the targeted state. Moreover, the actual perpetrator may spread false leads as to sponsorship. Even where the evidence is clearest, as when unimpeachable intelligence sources implicate the sponsoring state, the would-be retaliator may be unwilling to reveal the sources of that unimpeachable evidence or even the evidence itself, to anyone other than its closest allies. On the occasion of the bombing of Libya, President Reagan released extremely sensitive information that revealed a U.S. ability to monitor Libyan diplomatic communications, but this was highly unusual. Only some of the available evidence of Iraqi responsibility for an attempt to kill former President Bush was made public by President Clinton to justify the retaliatory strike against Baghdad in 1993.

There is no established answer to the central questions: what level of proof must be shown to whom and with what opportunity for rebuttal and when, if a retaliatory strike is to be justified against a state sponsoring terrorism? International law has only established that a military response cannot be used if a form of peaceful redress might work, that the military response must be proportional to the threat it addresses, and that it must impose the minimal damage necessary in carrying out its legitimate purposes.

Political issues intersect with the legal and moral ones. Great powers are far freer to act with less than conclusive evidence, and far freer to refuse to disclose their evidence publicly when responding to an act of terrorism they believe has been supported by another state. Great powers can decide, without fear of sanctions by the Security Council or responsive violence, how much sponsorship or tolerance is enough to warrant retaliation. And these decisions are generally made in the context of an inflamed public opinion and accompanying political demands for highly popular, muscular responses.

Nor is there equality in the selection of targets even by the United States. Some nations, the weak and diplomatically isolated, are relatively safe to attack. Others are more risky, due either to their strength or to their allies. This type of factor proved particularly significant before the collapse of the Soviet Union. The United States could retaliate against Libya far more easily and with far less risk than against Syria, which was almost an ally of the Soviet Union.

Concerns rooted in the uncertainties of international law and in the practicalities of foreign relations are often joined by moral qualms and fears of public reactions to slow the use of military retaliation. The death of noncombatants is a highly predictable result of military retaliation against a state that sponsors terrorism. The terrible and unintended civilian casualties of the Israeli attacks on Lebanese targets in the spring of 1996 make that point dramatically.

Does Retaliation Deter Terrorism? Does It Serve Other Purposes?

Whether a military strike will succeed in deterring a state from supporting terrorist attacks doubtless depends upon a number of factors. Sometimes it has; sometimes it will. But fully as often it has failed and will fail.

We are likely to overrate the prospects of deterring a smaller state's support for terrorism by attacking it militarily. The basic idea of deterrence makes almost irrefutable sense to American ears whether we are talking about the death penalty or a bombing strike. All we have to do is make it clear that the costs of continuing a course of activity will exceed the benefits, and it should stop. But it is not at all this simple.

In what ways might deterrence of a state that is a weaker military power fail, and how likely is this state of affairs? Consider the many possibilities. The state sponsoring terrorism may lack the capacity to stop the terrorist group. It may consider the actions necessary to stop the group more dangerous to the state's safety than the retaliatory strikes. The administration of the sponsoring state may find that the retaliatory strikes have political benefits, for example, uniting the public behind it. It may decide to continue sponsoring terrorist behavior but more secretly. The decisions about support for terrorist groups may be made by individuals or groups that enjoy the benefits of supporting terrorism without paying the full cost of retaliatory strikes, and these individuals or groups may not be fully controlled by the state's leadership.

The message sent by the retaliating state may not be clear. Even if it describes its actions as intended to deter future support for terrorism, the state sponsoring the terrorist activity may regard that as a ruse to cover other objectives of the retaliating state. Even if the message is clear, the sponsoring state may react with hatred and aggression rather than fear and submission, perhaps understanding the confrontation as challenging its very autonomy rather than a particular policy. In this, it may enjoy the support of allies, who applaud the bravery and steadfastness shown in standing up to a common enemy; this benefit may compensate for the costs of the strike. The strike may weaken internal political opposition to the main foreign policy directions, including hostility toward the retaliatory state, of the government. National pride is always a powerful incentive for a public.

How blame for the attack is attributed is critical. The population suffering the brunt of reprisal may blame the state that carried it out, or the terrorists whose actions evoked the punishment, or their own government for their anguish. Attribution of the blame is strongly influenced by the group affiliation of the victims of retaliation. For example, the Israeli hope in the spring of 1996 that Lebanese popular pressure would force the Syrian and Lebanese authorities to take stronger measures against the terrorists failed, because the Lebanese population blamed Israel, not the Hezbollah, with whom it more readily identified.

Doubtless there are other reasons why retaliation that appears promising on its face might fail or even backfire. My point is not to prove that retaliation to deter state sponsorship of terrorism will generally fail. It is simply to recognize that even without considering the possibility of irrational responses, a variety of perfectly rational reasons may defeat the specific deterrence that justifies, politically and legally, retaliatory military strikes. A decision to use a military response depends on more than the determination of the true responsibility for acts that are sometimes carefully hidden; on more than an assessment of the complicated moral questions raised by the likelihood of hitting innocent targets; and on more than difficult calculations of international law and international support. It also depends on a judgment of the prospects of being successful in terms of specific deterrence. And that obviously requires an intricate understanding of the culture, needs, goals, and politics of the target of retaliation.

History does not help resolve the questions about the effectiveness of military action in deterring state sponsorship of terrorism. In response to a bomb detonated in a Berlin discotheque on April 5, 1986 (killing two Americans and wounding sixty-two more), and pressed on by the Reagan administration's recent history of ever-stronger rhetoric, the United States launched Air Force and Navy fighter bombers against Libya. The targets were military, but incidental damage was done to a number of embassies and residences of ambassadors, and Libyan leader Muammar Qadhafi's one-year-old adopted daughter was killed. The response of Libya was either to reduce or to better disguise its support of terrorist attacks on American targets; no one is sure which. In the months that followed, Americans were the target of a number of attacks that may have been attributable to Libya. Bruce Hoffman, director of the Center for the Study of Terrorism and Political Violence, asserts that after a brief lull following the 1986 bombing of Libya by the United States, Libya not only resumed but actually increased its international terrorist activities.[2] A year after the raid, the U.S. State Department commented that "we had little doubt that the U.S. air raids on Libya in 1986 contributed heavily to Qadhafi's subsequent caution. At the same time, however, we are equally sure that he continued planning for anti-U.S. attacks involving the use of surrogate groups to disguise Libyan responsibility."[3] And American officials held Libyan officials responsible for the December 1988 bombing of Pan Am Flight 103 over Lockerbie, Scotland.

Similar difficulties of attribution, which are perhaps the result of greater care to maintain secrecy prompted by the U.S. military response, make difficult any conclusions as to the deterrent effect of President Clinton's attack on Iraq in 1993.

What is far clearer is the evidence of a boost in domestic morale and international influence following the military action. U.S. citizens do not want to feel powerless against the attacks of terrorist groups. In this, we are like almost every other nation—like, for example, the Israelis in their support of the actions of Israeli Prime Minister Shimon Peres against Hezbollah in the spring of 1996. In the aftermath of our bombing of Libya, only 30 percent of those interviewed by a *Washington Post*/ABC poll believed that our action would reduce terrorism, but 76 percent approved of the bombing.

According to the *New York Times*, President Clinton's retaliation against Iraq for the attack on former President Bush was equally popular.

These two U.S. raids also prevented the undermining of U.S. leadership on the issue of terrorism among our allies. Instead of looking too muscle-bound to deal with the subtle tactics of Libya or Iraq, the United States took bold, aggressive, and—to our allies—frightening responses. Our major allies, which in 1986 had only recently refused to join in imposing sanctions on Libya, changed their minds. Part of the reason was surely to prevent further military steps, which our allies would have regarded as reckless. But part was also the determination and commitment shown by the willingness of the United States to act alone.

Such intangible benefits of retaliation are not special to the Libyan case. President Clinton reaped them with his attack on Baghdad. Israel has sought and enjoyed such benefits over the decades that it has retaliated against Arab terrorist attacks, even without any evidence that its actions were in fact deterring the states sponsoring terrorism, rather than simply making them more cautious in disguising state responsibility.

Conclusion

In the final analysis, the fear of retaliation by the United States will, in some cases, deter the support for terrorism that would otherwise be a very inexpensive form of aggression by a hostile nation. But the United States is more likely to exaggerate the impact than to underrate it. There are many plausible reasons and a good deal of historic evidence to demonstrate that frequently a military response will not deter a state from sponsoring terrorism.

Although such specific deterrence is the only internationally accepted justification for a military response, it is not the only motivation. Democratic leaders find responding forcefully essential to the morale of their citizens and sometimes important to the credibility of the nation in foreign affairs. The threat of further military response has also proved a stimulus to the cooperation among allies that is necessary for effective economic, diplomatic, and travel sanctions against a state sponsoring terrorism. Such sanctions require difficult decisions of allies, but decisions that are less difficult than those presented by military action by the United States.

The inevitable confusion about underlying facts, the lack of clarity of international law, the certainty of civilian casualties, and the general uncertainty of deterrence should create a strong preference for economic, diplomatic, and travel sanctions rather than military action to deter a state supporting a terrorist group. Unilateral military action must, however, remain an option when the alternative is a free shot at the United States and its citizens by a hostile nation.

Chapter 6

Prevention of Terrorism: An Overview

Prevention provides a bridge between a focus on international terrorism in the preceding chapters and attention to domestic terrorism in the chapters that follow—between Mahmud Abouhalima of the World Trade Center bombing and Timothy McVeigh of the bombing of the federal building in Oklahoma City. The logic of prevention is the same at home or abroad; only the available tools differ. I begin by describing that logic and applying it to the forms of catastrophic terrorism with international roots that we have most reason to fear. Then I apply the same logic of prevention to more conventional forms of terrorism that may or may not have international connections.

The Role, Categories, and Logic of Prevention

The normal tools of law enforcement—arrest, prosecution, and imprisonment—are a powerful form of prevention of most crimes. The punishment of perpetrators deters others who would be tempted to engage in the same conduct, and discourages the perpetrators from doing it again. Incapacitation by imprisonment reduces the number outside prison walls who are willing and able to commit the crime. Punishment reinforces the social morality that is the major deterrent for many of us. For individuals ready to engage in terrorism for reasons of passionately held ideology or deeply felt resentment, the force of conventional, social morality may be weak and even the fear of punishment may have little impact. Still, we are dealing with small groups, and incapacitation can significantly affect the number able and willing to stay the course.

Why, then, do we not rely on the processes of law enforcement alone to maintain law and order in the case of terrorist bombings, as we do with street robberies or even the great majority of murders? The answer is because of the degree of harm that may be done before any arrest is made. For example, in the case of catastrophic terrorism, using nuclear, biological, or, with lesser danger, chemical weapons, catching the perpetrators after the event is obviously not our most important goal.[1] The same may be true with more conventional terrorism involving the bombing of planes or buildings. We cannot accept such harm if there are other ways, consistent with our commitment to civil liberties, to prevent the terrorist event. And there are.

THE CATEGORIES OF TARGETED AND UNTARGETED PREVENTION

Prevention can be "targeted" or "untargeted." Prevention is targeted if intelligence has enabled the government to identify the time and place of a proposed attack (as in the case of the earlier plan by the World Trade Center terrorists to assassinate President Hosni Mubarak of Egypt) or even to identify the individuals who are planning a terrorist strike (as in the case of their plans to bomb the Holland Tunnel in the aftermath of the World Trade Center bombing). The steps of targeted prevention are straightforward: isolate the target from the terrorists (or the terrorists from the target) or sabotage their plans; then arrest the terrorists as soon as you have exploited all the possibilities for determining their plans, associates, and supporters. The crucial ingredient is intelligence.

The government must have an adequate amount of information to take the steps of targeted prevention. Sometimes the amount of information needed for preventive steps is determined by legal or moral requirements. Under present rules in the United States, using arrest to separate a suspect, even of terrorism, from his target requires "probable cause" to believe he has committed that crime or is conspiring or attempting to commit that crime. Even if he can be arrested, he cannot be held beyond a reasonably prompt trial date unless he can be convicted beyond a reasonable doubt of an offense.

The danger of terrorist acts by those who cannot be held under those terms has seemed excessive to Israel and the United Kingdom; they have, therefore, enacted internment provisions that do not require conviction of a crime. But the United States has rarely subjected its citizens to such provisions and the memory of those few occasions (e.g., the confinement of Japanese-Americans to camps during World War II) is a bitter one.

We can, will, and do deport or exclude aliens on far less grounds and evidence than are required for conviction. Under the 1990 amendments to the Immigration and Nationality Act, an individual can be excluded and deported from the United States if he or she has either engaged in terrorist activity himself or herself or provided material support to someone else "in conducting a terrorist act." The Antiterrorism Act of 1996 extended the exclusion provision and denied political asylum rights to members of any group designated as "a foreign terrorist organization" by the secretary of state. It is now enough that the alien knows that the organization to which he or she belongs has terrorism among its activities for that alien to be excluded.

In exclusion proceedings, the alien has the burden of showing he or she is entitled to be in the United States. In deportation proceedings, the government must prove that the alien is deportable, but not by proof beyond a reasonable doubt. An alien is entitled to basic due process guarantees in deportation proceedings, including adequate conditions to confront and rebut the basis for the government's claim of a right to deport. But proceedings to exclude someone who has not been admitted to the United States require far fewer protections even than deportation under the Constitution.

Whether or not the suspect is an alien, information that is not adequate to convict or even arrest someone suspected of planning terrorism may be more than enough to justify monitoring his activities and those of an organization that seems to have the same aims. That in itself greatly increases the probability of stopping a member of the group before he or she can commit a dangerous act. If the monitoring reveals the target, the target can be protected. If the monitoring reveals the occasion, the occasion can be changed or provided with unusual protection.

With information so valuable to the government, much of pre-vention takes the form of devising methods to obtain more informa-tion. Some methods do not require changing laws. The gathering of information from a range of government agencies into the hands of a single lead agency, the FBI, was one objective of the Antiterrorism Act of 1996. The use of computers to draw conclusions from large amounts of apparently unrelated information is another major step in processing efficiently what is already being acquired.

The dangers and fears of terrorism have led other countries to expand their governments' powers to obtain necessary information. In Great Britain, it has been made a crime to fail to provide informa-tion about a terrorist event, and laws have made it possible to detain suspects for interrogation to gather information about others. Britain also broadened its powers of search and then used those broader powers in massive hunts for evidence and weapons. The United States has taken none of those steps, although it has expanded somewhat its willingness to infiltrate groups that preach violence.

When a nation lacks the intelligence for targeting suspects for arrest or surveillance or, in the case of aliens, exclusion, prevention necessarily takes a more general form. The purpose is to make it more risky and difficult to carry out a bombing or other terrorist act and thereby to reduce the level of terrorist events by, at a minimum, increasing the time, expense, and effort for each, and perhaps also reducing what may be a very limited total pool of participants by discouraging beginners, increasing defections, and incapacitating the firmly committed.

The desired effects of such untargeted prevention on the terrorist organization are both short-term and long-term. In the short term, the effort is to deny the terrorists materials, safe movement of people and materials, and necessary information about access to the target. To do so, the government must first identify what materials, move-ments of people and materials, access, and information the more likely terrorist groups would need to carry out the more likely categories of events. That is, it must develop a list of the steps the terrorist group would probably find necessary. Then, second, the government uses a variety of prohibitions, regulations, and information-gathering techniques at each likely step of the process of carrying out the terrorist event.

Prohibition and regulation are designed to make it less likely or more costly in time, expense, and effort to obtain what the terrorist group needs at any stage. Monitoring is designed to develop the many bits of information that can then be combined by sophisticated analysts with sophisticated equipment to identify suspects likely enough to be made the subjects of targeted prevention.

Assume, for example, that the conviction of Sheik Abdel-Rahman for the World Trade Center bombings raises particular fears of a retaliatory strike by supporters in Egypt using explosives against U.S. law enforcement, most likely in Washington or New York. Such a strike would require getting the necessary materials and, if they are obtained abroad, bringing them into the United States. It would also involve the movement of supporters into the United States. The United States would not want to close its borders completely to movements of goods or people, but it could greatly increase the vigilance with which it checks border crossings. The explosives might be bought in the United States, a step that could not be generally forbidden because there are so many legitimate uses for explosives. Still, an information-gathering effort to identify unusual purchases or stockpiling or movements of explosives can start to move untargeted prevention into a more productive targeted form.

All of these short-term steps of untargeted prevention are designed to complicate the task of terrorists, whoever they may be. Overcoming the difficulties and risks imposed by short-term prevention requires the terrorist to obtain outside assistance. Longer-term untargeted prevention is designed to deny terrorist groups that assistance by such measures as reducing the size of the overall pool of potential recruits by showing that terrorism is unlikely or unnecessary to achieve their objectives and by making clear the severity and likelihood of punishment; discouraging or denying (for example, by undercover operations) opportunities to safely recruit from whatever pool is available; and reducing the group's capacity to obtain material assistance from sympathizers.

A CLOSER LOOK AT THE LOGIC OF PREVENTION

The government's task of preventing terrorism is carried out by a set of actions that can disrupt, or make more difficult or costly or risky, a plan to bomb, take hostages, or assassinate. The logic of these forms of interference is clear, although complicated. It begins with the task of the terrorist. To accomplish his ends, the terrorist needs to: (a) locate the target, (b) get to it, (c) with the needed associates, (d) with the necessary information, equipment, and facilities, and (e) with an expectation of enough safety to justify taking the risks, in light of his or her dedication to whatever the goals of the terrorist act may be. Prevention of terrorism requires depriving the terrorist of one or more of these five conditions.

Most obviously, the pre-event arrest, conviction, and incapacitation behind prison walls (and far from their target) of critical members of the terrorist group will block conditions "b" and "c." In some countries arrest and conviction are not necessary. Because the amount of information required for these is so hard to accumulate, Northern Ireland and Israel allow internment without conviction and with much less proof. Alternatively, separation of the terrorists from their target can be accomplished by maintaining secrecy about the movements of the target or by limiting access to it (thus thwarting "a" or "b"). Even if access is generally allowed, policing on or shortly before the intended occasion of a terrorist act may, by prompt reaction, prevent the steps—for example leaving a bomb-filled bag in place until it explodes or drawing a weapon and shooting at close range— necessary to accomplish the act ("b") or to do so safely ("e").

The last condition, "e"—the willingness of the terrorist to take the risks of capture or death—can be affected by increasing those risks or at least appearing to do so. Any steps that convey the impression that the terrorist will certainly be caught, or that his or her colleagues may be cooperating or planning to cooperate with the police, will affect that willingness. The anticipation of widespread public condemnation of acts under consideration can also affect that willingness. (This helps explain why there has not yet been terrorism using biological weapons.) A sense that the terrorist act itself is unlikely to accomplish its objective will also discourage the perpetrators.

As to "d," the government can seek to control access to the information, materials, and facilities needed for the terrorist action. A terrorist group that does not know how to make a nuclear or biological weapon or cannot obtain the required uranium or anthrax will not engage in these forms of catastrophic terrorism. A terrorist group that cannot safely find living and working quarters in the target country is not a danger. Their inability to build bombs safely led to the arrests of two would-be terrorists in New York during the summer of 1997 and to the arrest of the central figure in the World Trade Center bombing, Ramzi Yousef, in Manila in 1996. In both cases mishaps revealed the enterprise. Government agents can and have substituted harmless powders or inoperable detonators for explosives, as recently as in the conspiracies to blow up the Holland Tunnel between New York City and New Jersey in 1993.

When information, materials, or facilities of the sort needed by terrorists are also used by others for legitimate purposes, access to them cannot be denied absolutely. Still, access can be regulated or it can be monitored and recorded, leaving a record that, as the terrorist knows, increases the likelihood of discovery and punishment, thus discouraging participation. Many believe that one such step would be to require identifying "taggants" in all explosives, which allow tracing, even after explosion, to the source of the materials.[2]

Finally, for "a," "b," "c," and "d," terrorists often need human support from sympathizers, even if the latter are unwilling to take the risks that the terrorists themselves are taking. Sympathizers can help provide safe access to information, materials, and facilities. They can also provide the encouragement needed for "e." They can provide warning of dangers or advice as to safe steps. In a variety of ways, governments can attempt to prevent these forms of support.

Applying the Logic to Nuclear and Biological Terrorism

There is no way of estimating persuasively what level of resources the United States should commit to the prevention of catastrophic forms of terrorism involving nuclear or biological weapons. We can estimate the damage, and it would be terrible. But we cannot judge the likelihood of a serious threat to use such weapons. We, fortunately, have not had such occasions. Still, the extreme danger of the threat suggests that there should be serious efforts of prevention. But what would the steps be?

NUCLEAR THREATS

Knowledgeable experts such as Professor Graham Allison, director of the Belfer Center for Science and International Affairs at Harvard's Kennedy School of Government, regard nuclear terrorism as the most serious security threat facing the United States today. The other catastrophic weapon that may become available to terrorists is biological. Professor Allison points out that the United States is spending a disproportionately tiny amount of its defense budget on what may be its single greatest threat, nuclear terrorism.

Despite a history of terrorists resorting to catastrophic weapons only on rare occasions, it seems madness to ignore any preventive steps that can be taken in these areas. The bombers of the World Trade Center were obviously prepared to bring about catastrophic damage. The same was true of the Aum Shinrikyo organization, which used sarin gas in Tokyo's subways. The very success of target democracies in remaining calm in the face of familiar levels of terrorism and in combating these over time may encourage terrorists to cross traditional lines of restraint.

What can and must be done requires specific detail well beyond the scope of this book. But the logic that explains the recommendations of the experts is exactly that set forth earlier in this chapter. Consider nuclear terrorism first. One path is targeted prevention, beginning by trying to identify any group that could combine the capacity and the willingness to carry out such an attack on the United States and then trying to penetrate the group by informants or other devices for intelligence. When the group's actions make it possible and not dangerously premature (in terms of knowing enough about its membership and plans), this path leads to convicting and incapacitating its members. The available intelligence could prevent the use of any catastrophic weapon either by seizing and disabling the weapon or by permitting arrests and seizures at the right time.

International cooperation may be crucial for information or arrest, but may not be available if the terrorists enjoy the support of a hostile state providing sanctuary, equipment, transportation, and security to the group.

Where intelligence does not permit such targeted prevention, the strategy has to be untargeted prevention. For example, to be capable of executing a nuclear explosion, a terrorist group has to have the necessary weapon or explosive device, be able with moderate safety to transport it to a threatened location, and have the capacity to hide it there if necessary. At each step, the object of untargeted prevention is to make the effort as difficult, expensive, and risky as possible.

In the case of the threat of nuclear terrorism, it is simplest to work backwards. An explosive device could be manageable in size once it has been assembled: a van or small truck could put it in place for detonation with only a small prospect of detection. The necessary fissile material for making the bomb would be far smaller than the bomb and could be smuggled into the United States as easily as drugs. As Graham Allison points out, "technologies designed to detect nuclear materials operate over very short ranges and are presently used only at secure storage facilities and by a few special search teams."[3]

Obviously there is only one crucial step that is difficult for the terrorists: obtaining the necessary device in the first place. This could be accomplished in three ways. A nuclear bomb could be purchased or stolen. Alternatively, one could be made if the terrorists could get their hands on the necessary fissile material (about one hundred pounds of highly enriched uranium or about half that weight in plutonium). Finally, a conventional explosive could be mixed with far more readily available radioactive materials (e.g., radioactive cobalt or strontium) to produce a radiological hazard that, while not as devastating as a nuclear explosion, would be terrifying and very dangerous. Consider only the most dangerous of likely alternatives: terrorists making their own crude atomic bomb.

It is widely agreed that if a terrorist group can obtain the necessary fissile material, they may be able to turn it into a nuclear weapon. More than twenty years ago, John Foster, a former director of the Lawrence Livermore Nuclear Laboratory, declared, "the only difficult thing about making a fission bomb of some sort is the preparation of a supply of fissile material of adequate purity; the design of the bomb itself is relatively easy."[4] The technology of bomb manufacturing once the needed materials are in hand, while relatively difficult to execute, is widely understood.

What is extremely difficult is to make bomb-usable material. Uranium-235 is only 0.7 percent of uranium found naturally, so to get fissile material, you have to create it, and most present stores are guarded and tracked. (There is, however, a large amount of non-fissionable, radioactive material, usually waste from reactors, that is unaccounted for in this or other countries. A competent bomb builder could attach it to a conventional bomb and contaminate a large area with radioactive residue.)

There is one massive source of fissionable, weapon-grade material in the world today that is very poorly guarded: the remnants of the arsenal of the former Soviet Union (and also the remnants of its nuclearization of power). Moreover, we now know of a number of efforts to sell and buy from that store.[5] Worst of all, the Russian storehouses for fissile material are poorly guarded and defended in a country where even the best of defenses would have to face the severe risks posed by corruption because law and order has broken down and black markets have grown up for everything imaginable.

Prevention of nuclear terrorism should, like all prevention, focus on the steps in the terrorist plan that can be made most difficult at a reasonable cost: obtaining the fissile material (as well, of course, as preventing the theft or sale of nuclear weapons themselves). We must continue and improve our methods of assisting Russia and other former Soviet republics to increase physical protection of their nuclear materials. We must be prepared to use undercover offers, as the Germans have done, to detect and disrupt black market activities. We must be prepared to buy loose materials, as we did when a thousand pounds of highly enriched uranium was found in Kazakhstan. We must, as Graham Allison argues, promote a long-term management plan for "coping with the global surplus of excess fissile material."[6]

BIOLOGICAL DANGERS

The same logic would apply to the quite different problem of terrorism with biological weapons, the destructiveness of which could be comparable to a small nuclear device. Professor Matthew Meselson of Harvard's Department of Molecular and Cellular Biology is the expert on whom I rely in illustrating the logic of prevention here.[7] I begin again with what terrorists would have to do to use biological weapons.

A biological weapon operates by spreading an infectious, living agent (e.g., a virus) through the use of a conventional, explosive or aerosol device. Biological weapons are broadly banned by international treaty. They create a horror that may stand as an initial barrier to a terrorist group seeking to use them. They are novel, different, and extremely dangerous. So the first task of a group wanting to use this weapon would be to overcome this horror among its own members or its suppliers.

It could obtain a biological weapon from a country that was secretly producing one. Iraq would be a possibility. Or it could build the device itself. The starting place of prevention is to think of the steps that it would have to take along each of these paths. Let us follow the path of creating a weapon itself. It is hard to isolate pathogens. The task requires considerable technical sophistication. A terrorist group would thus be more likely to order or otherwise obtain pathogens from those providing them for legitimate purposes and then grow and perhaps dry the products, depending on the intended method of dissemination. There is some danger in the process.

The group would probably want to use a well-known pathogen such as anthrax, which offers the advantage of stability, experience in culturing and storing it, and certainty of results. But even then, a test might be necessary. The Japanese group Aum Shinrikyo apparently felt it wise to test its chemical (not biological) weapon at Matsumoto before using it in the subways of Tokyo.

The group would have to maintain complete secrecy during this process and during the ensuing steps of delivery. The problem of delivery is that the pathogen must be in an aerosol form—that is, its particles must be small enough (less than 50 microns) to remain hovering in the air where it can be breathed. The aerosol particles must also be small enough, perhaps less than 10 microns, to get into the lungs in order to produce widespread infection. The terrorist group would need the equipment to produce and deliver this aerosol. Commercial devices are available that would allow deliveries of small amounts of the biological weapon. To deliver large amounts, the equipment would be more unusual, perhaps like that used with some agricultural insecticides, and modified in certain respects.

If the purpose of the group required it first to threaten the use of the weapon in an effort to obtain some concession, it would have to find a way to prove that it was not bluffing. If it were to carry out the threat, maximum effect would require a mobile delivery vehicle to carry the dispersing equipment in a major city, releasing it along a crosswind line upwind of the intended target area.

Now, let us return to the opportunities for prevention. First, through a variety of devices we can try to maintain the broad barrier to this new form of destruction. That is, we can try to build the reluctance of any members of a terrorist group to take part, or their willingness to take the steps that would block such efforts by their terrorist colleagues. The use of biological weapons should be made a universal offense triable in any country. The United States can make clear its full commitment to preventing use anywhere, by anyone, private or governmental. Rewards for information could be offered, preferably by the United Nations because of its neutrality.

If the first line of defense, making terrorists unwilling to use this form of weapon, failed, a second line of defense of making it risky and difficult should follow. As to delivery by rogue nations of a fully developed weapon, the promise of retribution must be strong and sure. Beyond that, work must continue on the extremely difficult task of detecting national efforts to build biological weapons, despite the fact that needed installations may be small and that many of the ingredients have a legitimate use as well as a forbidden one (i.e., "dual-use").

For the creation of biological weapons by a terrorist group itself, the preventive steps follow the steps it would have to take. We should make efforts to avoid publicizing the technology of how to isolate pathogens and grow pathogens or produce them in a storable and lethal form. Terrorists may well seek to buy dual-use pathogens. The United States now tries to regulate such sales and transfers. We should also monitor their movement, by international intelligence-gathering devices as well as by domestic regulation, relaying information that is even somewhat suspicious (for example, about orders of pathogens that are rarely used) to a center whose responsibility it is to combine items of information that are only somewhat suspicious in an effort to find a pattern that is very suspicious.

The terrorists need secrecy and we should try to defeat that. Tips can be elicited by money as well as by moral outrage. Very large rewards, preferably through the United Nations as well as through our own government, should be available to anyone who reveals any effort to produce a biological weapon. The rewards have to be made widely known, as was the case of the reward for the arrest of the fugitives in Pakistan. The legitimate producers or users of dual-use equipment are also potential sources of information: they must be made aware of what to call to the attention of the government monitoring center. Particular types of fermenters and aerosol dispersing equipment, for example, may be suspect when acquired by particular individuals. Whom to call with suspicions must be widely known. A further source of information would be records of hospitals reporting cutaneous anthrax infection or other infections associated with making a biological weapon.

As to the mechanisms of dispersal of aerosols, monitoring and perhaps markers would be useful. It is harder to imagine how we could regulate or monitor delivery of dispersal systems; dispersal could be done by a vehicle as small as a normal automobile. The U.S. military was able to carry out, apparently without detection, hundreds of tests of simulated chemical and biological weapons in the United States using such vehicles in the 1950s and 1960s.

Finally, prevention would also include decisions as to how we would recognize a credible threat, what form of guarantee of no repetition would be part of any concession, and what we would do to minimize the damage in the event that a biological weapon was released.

A Closer Look at the Prospects of Some Major Tactics to Prevent Conventional Terrorist Attacks

The United States can try to keep potential terrorists who are not citizens away from all targets within the United States by immigration controls, that is, by exclusion or deportation. We can also try to keep those within our borders away from the most likely or tempting targets of terrorism. These are the two "separating" devices that other Western nations faced with terrorism have also used. Neither promises dramatic success, but each may be useful.

The usefulness of immigration controls depends upon the prediction that a high proportion of terrorists acting against the United States are likely not to be U.S. citizens. In recent decades the most frequent objective of terrorists attacking U.S. citizens and property has been to change the foreign policy of the United States. The perpetrators of terrorism for this purpose are often citizens of some other nation and thus not entitled to enter or remain in the United States, except as permitted by statute.

Through our own intelligence-gathering efforts or through liaison with foreign intelligence agencies, the United States could identify a number of people who are likely to have been engaged in politically motivated violence. When Sheik Abdel-Rahman came to the United States from Egypt, three years before the effort to blow up the World Trade Center and other buildings in New York, he was on a list of such people. This was also true of the sheik's associate, Ramzi Yousef, when he entered in September 1992.

As a practical matter, the effectiveness of deportation and exclusion depend on the intelligence on which they are based. And even this measure of effectiveness is limited by the possibility that an individual known to be a terrorist can enter our country surreptitiously or openly under false identity, or even by bureaucratic slip-up, as happened with Sheik Abdel-Rahman.[8]

Individuals already within the United States enjoy an almost unbounded freedom to travel. Still, we can rule certain potential targets "out of bounds" to all who do not have a need to be there. The central problem is that the number of potential targets is often extremely large. At the federal level, the Executive Branch is housed in approximately seven thousand buildings. We can protect the White House from trucks and cars so long as we are willing to bar traffic on Pennsylvania Avenue near 16th Street. But protecting all of the Executive Branch buildings would be prohibitively expensive, whether the effort was to use guards, inanimate barriers, or sophisticated electronic detection systems. And even if we could protect all seven thousand federal buildings from vehicular attack, attack from the air would remain possible. And the federal buildings are only a tiny fraction of the total attractive targets for bombing.

One particular type of target has enjoyed unique protection. At considerable expense, we have become very successful in protecting air traffic in the United States against hijackers. The attractiveness of commercial airplanes as targets suggests that we should be providing similar protection against bombs in checked luggage, even if the cost would be substantial. The 1996 legislation that instructs the administrator of the Federal Aviation Authority to require foreign carriers serving airports in the United States to comply with the same security measures as American carriers will not protect us unless the administrator makes the standards high enough for both groups.

Bombings are not the only problem. The same issue of difficulty and expense in protecting each one of a multiplicity of attractive targets is true of officials at risk of assassination. We do provide protection for our highest officials, and for others when the threat is known. The 1996 Antiterrorism Act makes federal crimes of a variety of attacks on officials. But we could not systematically protect all likely targets of assassination, let alone a crowd of otherwise unknown travelers such as those Americans machine-gunned a decade ago in airports in Rome and Vienna.

More than expense is involved. Democracy depends, to a considerable extent, on the access of ordinary citizens to government facilities and personnel. Denying this access is necessary for substantial physical protection, but carries a price in distancing citizens from their government. That price is worth paying to protect particularly critical facilities, such as nuclear weapons storage sites, and people, such as the president or the secretary of state. But to go much further is to become a garrison state, and, even then, we could not provide reliable protection for ordinary people against the familiar tools of terrorism: assassination, bombing, and hostage-taking.

In short, physical security measures are helpful in protecting selected targets but not in preventing terrorism altogether. That has been the experience of the United Kingdom, which built little fortresses to protect British military bases in Northern Ireland; Italy and Germany, which made their courts for trying terrorists into bunkers; and France, which could not end waves of bombing in 1986 and the mid-1990s. Expense creates limits to this strategy. We have spent several billions of dollars to protect our embassies abroad, but we must recognize the limits that expense imposes to the use of physical barriers as a response to terrorism.

DENYING RESOURCES AND INFORMATION

One particular way of denying terrorists the special capacities they need merits special mention: making it difficult for them to obtain or to keep secret their acquisition of unusually dangerous weapons. Restricting access to attractive explosives and to the materials for nuclear, biological, and chemical weapons, and keeping track of those who have had such access, are important steps of prevention. An international convention requires that detectant agents be placed in all plastic explosives. Federal criminal statutes now enforce that requirement. The 1996 Antiterrorism Act makes it a crime to transfer any explosive materials to another "knowing or having reasonable cause to believe" that they will be used to commit a crime of violence.[9] Federal statutes already prohibit the acquisition, possession, or use of biological weapons. The 1996 Act makes a federal crime of the use of chemical weapons within the United States or against Americans outside of the United States.

Access to information and training can be equally important. British law forbids paramilitary training and instruction in the use of firearms or explosives unless for sporting, industrial, or other bona fide purposes. In the United States we continue to allow uninhibited dissemination of information about how to make bombs and how to kill individuals. A Department of Justice report submitted to the Congress in April 1997 assessed the availability of the most dangerous information and concluded that "anyone interested in manufacturing a bomb, dangerous weapon, or weapon of mass destruction can easily obtain detailed instructions for fabricating and using such a device. . . . [S]uch information is [not only in manuals but] readily available to anyone with access to a home computer equipped with a modem." Indeed, the First Amendment of the Constitution prevents efforts to block the flow of such information in most cases. The sole exception urged by the Department of Justice is for conveying such information with the intent that it be used violently and illegally or with the knowledge that a particular recipient has such an intent.[10]

This aspect of U.S. protection of dangerous speech by terrorists is important. Not knowing how to make a bomb or how to kill in other ways is another obstacle to terrorism by isolated individuals or very small groups at the faraway fringes of American society. The public availability of instruction removes that barrier. In allowing this, we doubtlessly pay a real price for our traditional protection of even outrageous speech.

DENYING TERRORISTS THE SUPPORT THEY NEED FROM OTHERS
To engage in any of the classic forms of political violence—bombing, assassination, or hostage-taking—let alone to attempt something far more sophisticated, those carrying out the action need help in a variety of ways from supporters. They need secure communications; safe houses for themselves, material, and hostages; necessary equipment such as cars and explosives; false identity papers and license plates; money for transportation; and much more by way of material support. They need crucial information about such matters as how to make a bomb or the movements of police or the design of a targeted

facility or the daily schedule of a government leader. Still less tangibly, they need the moral support of others to sustain the morale of their present members and the willingness of others to join. Denying terrorists or potential terrorists these forms of support is the second major form of prevention long used by Western governments and now pursued by the United States as well.

One source of such support to a terrorist organization is a foreign state. The Antiterrorism Act of 1996 contains a number of measures designed to discourage this. It is now a federal crime for any U.S. citizen knowingly to engage in a financial transaction with a country that has been designated as supporting international terrorism by the secretary of state. The secretary of the treasury must oppose a loan to any such state from any of the major international financial institutions. The president is empowered to withhold assistance from the government of any country that provides assistance to a state that the secretary of state has found aids terrorism. No defense article or defense service can be sold for export to a country that the president determines is not cooperating fully with United States antiterrorism efforts. Assistance is authorized for foreign countries who need help in their counter-terrorism efforts.

Another source of such support is sympathizers within the United States. The Antiterrorism Act of 1996 empowers the secretary of state, after consultation with the secretary of the treasury and the attorney general, to designate any foreign organization as one that engages in "terrorist activity" threatening to the security of U.S. nationals or the national security of the United States. Individuals are forbidden from rendering any form of assistance to such international terrorist organizations. For any person to raise funds for such a designated foreign terrorist organization is made a serious crime. Financial institutions are forbidden to dispense these funds, and are required to notify the secretary of treasury that they have them. An organization so designated is entitled to judicial review within 30 days after being notified of its designation, although the judge may authorize the attorney general to reveal privately to the court particular information whose disclosure would pose a risk to national security.

The 1996 Act goes beyond making it criminal to knowingly provide any form of material support or resources to a designated foreign terrorist organization or to assist a terrorist crime. Other provisions—making racketeering and money-laundering statutes applicable to terrorist offenses—broaden the prohibitions against knowing support, and add asset forfeiture and other serious penalties.[11]

Certain steps central to the Antiterrorism Act of 1996—both in its prohibitions of support of foreign terrorist organizations and in its effort to prevent foreign terrorists from entering or remaining in the United States—require an administrative determination that particular foreign organizations are terrorist. They therefore raise two questions of political liberty.

First, they apply to organizations which may have legitimate purposes, as long as they also have illegitimate, terrorist purposes. Still, it is not too much to ask of an organization seeking support for its non-violent activities that it abandon violence as a condition of receiving that support. Nor is it too much to ask of a supporter of legitimate activities that he find an organization prepared to further these activities without also using violence.

The second problem is potentially more serious. It is a dangerous step to prohibit a political organization from receiving support simply on the determination that it is a terrorist organization by a cabinet official whose factual determinations can be overturned by a court only if they are "arbitrary, capricious, [or] an abuse of discretion." That the law applies only to foreign organizations reduces significantly the danger to our domestic liberties, yet in an increasingly international world, foreign organizations play an increasing part in our politics as well. In earlier years, the African National Congress (ANC) of Nelson Mandela would have been subject to such prohibitions if the secretary of state had said so; even now, the law could apply to the political arms of the Irish Republican Army, depending very largely on the discretion of a cabinet officer reversible only if his judgment is arbitrary.

In choosing such measures, we follow a path taken with some success by Britain in its long battle with the Irish Republican Army.

Under Britain's Prevention of Terrorism Act of 1987, any real or personal property that is made available to a proscribed organization can be seized if the owner had "reasonable cause" to believe it was to be used by that organization. This form of support is also a crime, and investigators are given extensive access to financial records to investigate the IRA's finances. Most experts believe that since the Act took effect, prosecutions for financial offenses have dealt a significant blow to the IRA.

In two ways, however, the United Kingdom has gone much further than the United States is prepared to go in denying support to terrorists: first, Britain made it a crime to publicly encourage political violence; second, it has proscribed membership in named organizations. Britain has forbidden the wearing of badges and uniforms supportive of terrorist groups and has prosecuted IRA supporters for selling propaganda supportive of the IRA and for arranging meetings. The British government also banned the broadcasting of "the words of any speaker" who claimed to be a spokesman for the IRA or who supported terrorism. More effective still was the issuance of informal guidance to the British Broadcasting Corporation to portray the IRA unsympathetically and to support the government's positions relatively uncritically.

Such steps are unlikely in the United States. In 1969, in the case of *Brandenburg v. Ohio*,[12] the U.S. Supreme Court found unconstitutional steps similar to those taken by Great Britain, and declared encouragement of Ku Klux Klan violence to be constitutionally protected free speech, unless the violence was threatened imminently. The inability of the United States, under the Bill of Rights, to adopt such measures—at least until the need and demand for them is made very great and clear and urgent by a wave of terrorism—has important consequences. Terrorism can take many forms, but one quite likely threat in the United States is that posed by the inevitable existence, in a country of well over a quarter of a billion people, of at least a handful of individuals like Timothy McVeigh who are so angry at the government or society as to undertake politically motivated violence. The lack of social support for any such action—the social condemnation that certainly awaits any act of violent terrorism—provides something of a wall of deterrence that adds support to the criminal law. But speeches or writings by charismatic leaders urging political violence can provide the battering ram of encouragement a potential terrorist needs to take himself past the wall of social condemnation to a willingness to commit violent acts.[13]

However, there is little evidence that the British effort to control speech has been particularly effective in controlling terrorism. And, at least as to encouraging terrorism, U.S. broadcasters have adopted their own guidelines. For example, ABC specifies that:

Demands of the terrorist(s) should be reported as an essential ingredient of the story. But we must avoid becoming a platform for propaganda and rhetoric. In most cases, this means we will condense, edit or paraphrase the demands and explain the background against which they are made.[14]

This is a far cry from the days immediately after the U.S. embassy staff in Iran was taken hostage in November 1979. Then, Iranian officials used paid ads in American newspapers, entertainment of American reporters, and well-orchestrated "spontaneous" demonstrations in Iran to defend the hostage-taking. All three major networks rushed to interview the Ayatollah Khomeini, having agreed to submit their questions in advance and to broadcast the interview in prime time. Later, NBC conducted an interview with a hostage who was, in that circumstance, far from free to state his honest thoughts, and allowed Iranian militants several minutes of unedited air time.

Great Britain has also gone well beyond the United States by proscribing membership in, not just material support of, designated terrorist organizations. Other Western democracies, such as Italy, Germany, and Israel, have taken the same path to deny support to terrorist activities and, particularly in Germany, to facilitate prosecution of active terrorists. It is by no means clear that the U.S. Constitution permits prohibition of membership in a religious or political organization unless the member specifically intends to further the illegal goals of the organization. A series of decisions supporting freedom of association under the First Amendment suggests that membership in an organization that has both legal and illegal purposes cannot be proscribed without finding an intent, on a case-by-case basis, to support the illegal purposes.

One can easily exaggerate how much is sacrificed by the U.S. reluctance to punish membership alone. Our conspiracy laws are very broad. Any activity intentionally supportive of illegal acts by a terrorist organization could make the actor responsible for all the crimes carried out in furtherance of the organization's objectives as long as they were foreseeable. The anti-racketeering statute (RICO) would permit a single trial of all those who carried out or knowingly assisted at least two serious crimes on behalf of the organization.[15]

In any event, a prohibition of membership has great practical costs. Government ministers in the United Kingdom joined many others in regretting the loss of access to information about the activities of the IRA that came with efforts to limit its membership.

Avoiding the Providing of Encouragement to the Terrorist Organization

In two ways, a democratic government can unintentionally provide encouragement or support for an organization involved in terrorist attacks on its people and property. By complying with the demands of the terrorists, it can encourage them and others to engage in further acts of terrorism. Alternatively, by discriminating against an identifiable group of citizens of which the terrorists represent a radical fringe, it can reduce the reserve of loyalty and patriotism within this group and build a fund of hostility and fear, leading others to join the terrorist cause. Both risks can be illustrated by the experience of France under its then newly elected Prime Minister, Jacques Chirac, when, in the spring of 1986, he assumed responsibility for dealing with a frightening campaign of bombings concentrated in downtown Paris.

Chirac had campaigned in large part on the need to strengthen France's resistance to domestic and foreign terrorist groups. The terrorists responded with dramatic and terrifying bombings. They punctuated Chirac's inaugural address with a bombing at a crowded shopping mall, killing two and wounding twenty-eight. The bombing continued, and each attack was followed by a communiqué issued in Beirut by an organization that identified itself as the Committee for Solidarity with Arab and Middle Eastern Political Prisoners (CSAMPP). CSAMPP was originally believed to be a cover name for a small Christian Marxist terrorist group from Lebanon (FARL—the Lebanese Armed Revolutionary Factions), which had earlier claimed responsibility for several attacks on U.S. and Israeli diplomats in Paris. (See pp. 57–59 above.) The group was later determined to be a pro-Iranian cell group whose purpose was to obtain the release of Georges Ibrahim Abdallah, FARL's leader, whom France had arrested in 1984 for terrorist attacks. CSAMPP had no substantial support among any sizeable French group.

While the bombing campaign continued, Chirac's government sought to deny the terrorists the support of others by seeking legislative authority to expel from France, with few formalities, illegal residents from Arab countries. The example is important, for it is dangerous to focus repressive steps on the wider group from which a small terrorist group is likely to get support. This may very well alienate enough members of the wider group to greatly increase the likelihood of their support. Such a focus is, more broadly, likely to stimulate a process which can create severe divisions within society. This was a serious risk in France, where resentment against two million residents from Arab and African countries had led to the creation of a right-wing nationalist party, the National Front, under the leadership of Jean-Marie Le Pen, and had brought arbitrary attacks on people of Arab and African origin.

The United States could face the same issue with regard to its many very sizeable minority groups. In the three days following the Oklahoma City bombing in April, an anti-defamation group recorded 222 attacks against Muslims.[16] Many were minor, but not to their victims or the group to which they belonged. The more fundamental point is the immorality of holding American Muslims responsible for a crime in fact committed by people motivated by right-wing politics and in no way connected with the Islamic religion. But even as a matter of pragmatism, it would not make sense for the United States government to do anything to undermine the allegiance of its six million Muslim citizens. Focusing remedies on them, even if it had been a Middle Eastern group that carried out the terrorism, would be both unfair and dangerously counterproductive. Indeed, both morality and wisdom dictate stern government efforts to defend Muslim Americans, and to isolate the perpetrators of terrorism from the support of those who have at least some reason to feel alienated and threatened by the broader society.

Accommodation of the demands of a terrorist group is equally risky. Unable to stop the bombings in any other way, Prime Minister Chirac's government began giving hints in September 1986 that it was prepared to deal in some way with the group's insistence that Abdallah be freed or at least not punished severely. The Chirac government dealt with representatives of CSAMPP through Monsignor Capucci, a Catholic priest well-connected with Iran and Syria, and through the government's own connections with the secret police of Algeria and Syria. The government promised a "favorable" verdict when its courts came to try the Abdallah case.

The risks of such an accommodation strategy are obvious. Above all, it can encourage the terrorist group to escalate its demands and lead other groups to seek similar opportunities. A less obvious price is often to alienate other nations whose risks will become greater as a result of the accommodation. Great Britain and the United States, for example, saw that part of Chirac's accommodation involved denying its allies support for condemnation of Syrian efforts to blow up an El Al plane en route to Israel from London. Finally, an accommodation strategy may present the government as weak and subject to blackmail. Prime Minister Chirac's tactic made him vulnerable to biting attacks by the opposition Socialist Party and much of the French press.

Chirac was not alone in taking these risks. President Reagan generated all of these harms at much the same time by encouraging the transfer of missiles to Iran in the hope it would use its influence with terrorist groups in Lebanon to obtain the release of a handful of hostages. Although hostages were released, other Americans were taken hostage in equal numbers. The effort undermined, even demeaned, the effort of the United States to bring its allies to stand firm when their citizens were taken hostage. The final consequence—that the strategy presents the government as weak and subject to blackmail—was also true. The pathetic picture of the U.S. national security advisor carrying a birthday cake and a bible autographed by President Reagan to the Ayatollah Khomeini in Iran is one that sticks unpleasantly in many memories.

There is an inherent potential for conflict between efforts to reduce people's willingness to support a terrorist group and efforts to avoid making concessions that might make terrorism look like a useful tactic. Dealing constructively with the grievances of those who would form the natural allies of the terrorist group, because they would be most sympathetic to its cause, discourages support within the broader population of potential allies. But any action of this sort may also appear to be prompted by the terrorist attacks. If so, the credit and loyalty may go to the terrorist group, creating the least desired effect.

Conclusion

Law enforcement, the subject of the next chapter, is extremely important in dealing with terrorism, but it is far from enough. There is a logical approach to prevention, linking targeted and untargeted prevention measures, that can significantly reduce the danger that terrorist events will take place. In the case of catastrophic terrorism, systematic efforts at prevention are essential. As to acts of ordinary terrorism, attempts at prevention can be helpful, but must be balanced far more carefully against risks to civil liberties and risks of alienating significant portions of the population.

Chapter 7

Using the Criminal Justice System to Catch and Punish

It is obvious from the success of the World Trade Center investigation and of the related investigation of the conspiracy to bomb other sites in the New York area, the conviction of Timothy McVeigh for bombing the federal building in Oklahoma City, and the capture of the "Unabomber," Theodore Kaczynski, that the United States has been able to find evidence and prosecute terrorist bombings under existing rules for investigation and trial. In each case, massive resources have been directed to the solution of the crimes, but it has not been necessary to change the rules. In testimony before the Senate Judiciary Committee in July 1997, FBI Director Louis Freeh expressed confidence in our ability to solve terrorist crimes so long as the needed resources are committed.[1]

The investigation of the bombing of the World Trade Center is revealing. It started at the crime scene, in the crater the bomb created, with an army of meticulous searchers. The fact that there was already a joint terrorism task force in New York facilitated the cooperation of several federal and local agencies. Agents and officers talked to witnesses as quickly as they could be located. To reach out further, they immediately established hotlines and offered rewards. They asked the police to tell them of any arrests or traffic stops near the time of the explosion. They checked whether there had been any threatening calls or any other messages that might be revealing.

Then they turned to recorded information, from all the pay phones in the area, all the security video cameras scanning the area for banks or other businesses, and intelligence and law enforcement agencies who might have picked up something that could be helpful. They checked with informants and carefully looked for clues on tapes of any past electronic surveillance of groups that might have been responsible. Any physical evidence that might help was sent immediately to FBI laboratories and promptly processed. A tiny scrap of the rented vehicle was enough of a lead to enable the FBI to trace the vehicle to a rental agency, which in turn opened up a rapidly expanding treasury of leads. The case was solved by an intensive use of familiar investigative techniques.

Other countries, faced with far more serious and enduring campaigns, have changed the rules. As early as 1984, Christopher Hewitt's study on "The Effectiveness of Anti-Terrorist Policies" concluded that the one measure that seemed to work in reducing violence was the arrest or internment of terrorists.[2] His explanation was simply that terrorist losses cannot be made up easily by recruiting new members. Great Britain, Germany, Israel, and Italy all made changes in their criminal justice process during the 1980s in an effort to accomplish the dismantling of terrorist organizations. Three such changes have been particularly important. These nations have extended the powers of police to search, engage in electronic surveillance, and interrogate suspects. They have sought additional ways to protect witnesses against threats, even at the cost of increasing the risks of error or witness malice by doing away with important occasions for confrontation with the defendant. Finally, they have sought ways to protect the fact-finder—judge or jury—from intimidation. We should consider the need for these steps and their constitutionality in the United States. To do so requires an understanding of how an investigation works and, in particular, the special problems associated with investigating terrorist cases.

A Primer on Investigations

Consider a very simple form of investigation involving a non-terrorist bombing. Assume that Jones has decided to compete with several well-established haulers of trash, and that those who have tried to enter the business in the past have been threatened. A week later, two of his drivers are forced out of their trucks, which are then blown up.

The crucial investigative steps at this stage are obvious: the investigators question Jones and the drivers about the events surrounding the crime. This will generate information about competitors who are likely suspects. The investigators can then question other individuals about the activities of each of the competitors or its employees before, during, and after the occasion on which the crime occurred. Their aim is to find a fit between the facts of the offense and the recent history of one of the competitors or its employees, a fit that could hardly be coincidental.

The investigators will also question specific suspects; an unwillingness to describe their activities would confirm that the investigation is properly focused on them, a demonstrably false alibi would be strong evidence of guilt, and an admission would be nearly conclusive. The suspects can be presented to the drivers in a line-up. Probable cause to believe that evidence of a crime may be in a competitor's house or office will justify a search for physical evidence. Finally, because the present activities and conversations of the suspects may be highly probative of their past activities, surveillance by officers or informants might be considered. If there is probable cause, electronic surveillance might also be available.

This comparatively simple example provides a useful summary of most of the major sources of information to which the investigators can turn at any stage of any investigation: witnesses (including the victim) to the offense or to the offender's prior action; the suspects; any physical evidence linking suspects to the crime; and surveillance of their present activities or conversations. As additional sources of information, the investigators can often consult written records made by the suspect, another private party, or the government. They might also examine collected information on similar offenses and their perpetrators.

What is wanted from all these sources of information? The answer goes to the meaning of an investigation. Crimes, like any other human activity, tend to leave traces. Offenders, like anyone else, have individual histories that also leave traces. An individual has friends, relatives, and acquaintances who know what he looks like, when he was or was not in a particular place, whether he is employed or unemployed, and with whom he is generally seen. The investigators may know the names of individuals with records involving similar crimes. An individual who has committed a crime may have discussed it with others beforehand; he may talk to others in the future about it. If a large sum of money was taken, elevated levels of spending may leave a trace, as they did in 1998, leading to the solution of the largest armored truck robbery in U.S. history.[3]

Solving a crime requires finding a strongly persuasive mesh between the traces of an offense and the history of a particular individual. There are many ways to match traces of a crime obtained from one source with traces of personal history coming from another source. In the case of an unknown street robber who has fled the scene, the investigators may circulate a description, an artist's drawing, or a picture taken by a surveillance camera. They may invite the victim to look through a "mug book" containing the pictures of suspected robbers. They may talk to "fences" or informants who circulate in a world where discussions of robbery would likely take place or where traces of the proceeds would easily be recognized. The investigators may simply happen upon physical evidence in the course of performing other duties.

To detect the traces of any crime, the investigators have available only a limited set of steps that can be combined, in a more or less considered sequence, into a specific investigative plan. They may interview willing witnesses or seek to have unwilling witnesses testify under legal compulsion. They may question the suspect under more or less coercive conditions. They may view and analyze publicly available physical evidence or use legal authority to search in private places. They may review publicly available or voluntarily produced records or seek to have other records produced under legal compulsion. They may engage in physical or electronic surveillance of the suspect's activities. They may use informants or offer rewards. They may use undercover operations to have an agent appear to join in an ongoing conspiracy. This list would be about the same in any political system, because I have not included legal and administrative limitations on the police in the analysis.

The probability of successfully solving a crime is initially a function of several factors: the traces that are left by a particular crime and its perpetrator; the willingness of private individuals to call these traces to the attention of the investigators; the investigative resources (time, money, and equipment) devoted by officials to the particular crime; the intelligence with which the resources are used; and the activities that the investigators are permitted to engage in while using these resources. Of these factors, the investigators exercise some control only over the allocation and productive use of resources.

Two investigative settings are particularly problematic in terms of the factors determining the likelihood of success. In one such situation, the investigators cannot narrow the list of suspects in a way that will enable them to compare the personal histories of a limited number of suspects with the events known about the crime. This is a typical problem with home burglaries. In a second problematic setting, the investigators are aware of a crime and they even have a small list of possible suspects, but they are unable to obtain witnesses who will help resolve the matter and testify at trial. Organized crime cases are often of this sort. We should consider each of these categories, for they are very relevant to terrorist bombings.

INVESTIGATIVE SITUATIONS LACKING A RELATIVELY NARROW LIST OF SUSPECTS
Most people and organizations categorize information and memories in terms of known, identifiable individuals. If one imagined this entire set of memories being collected and filed centrally, one might picture an immense inventory of detailed information about individuals. Under each heading, there would be significant information about the personal history and characteristics of an individual. By systematically going through the histories of possible suspects, the investigators in this fantasy world could theoretically solve any reported crime if they had only a fair description of its circumstances.

The problem lies elsewhere. No one collects all this information centrally and, of course, there are many very good reasons why we would not want it to be collected. Even if it were collected, the task of reviewing all potentially pertinent files would be close to impossible if the investigators had merely a rough description of the perpetrator and the time and place of the crime.

A crucial step in solving any crime is to create "files" on suspected individuals that did not previously exist. To do so, investigators must isolate a relatively small group of suspects for whom traces of personal history, around the time of the crime, can be collected. Investigators, hoping to find a suggestive match, will have to compare what they know about the crime with law enforcement records, forensic evidence, and the memories of private individuals about the suspects. But, as a practical matter, they cannot create such files on more than a few individuals. In the easiest case, only a few individuals could have been present at the time of the crime or could have known of the particular criminal opportunity that was exploited. The case is far more difficult to solve and may not be worth pursuing if the number of individuals whose histories might match the traces of the crime is very large. The bombing at the hugely crowded Atlanta Olympics in 1996, long unsolved, is a good example.

The long career of the "Unabomber" is another reminder that it will be hard to usefully narrow the list of suspects in terrorist bombings for a number of reasons. When there is no announcement of the reason for the bombing, as was the case in Atlanta and in Oklahoma City, the possible motivations may be too numerous to even begin to limit the suspect category (although in the Oklahoma case, the fact that the explosion occurred on the anniversary of the Waco fire, and, in the Atlanta case, that there were several other bombings with very similar techniques did help narrow the field). Other ways of reducing the list of possible suspects are likely not to work either. Bombs can be put in place some indeterminate period of time before the explosion that first focuses attention on their presence, so it is less likely than with other crimes that someone will notice and remember who was present when the critical act—placing the bomb—took place. Finally, the explosion is likely to destroy many of the traces of whoever left the bomb.

On the other hand, there is one immense advantage in terrorist investigations. The fear and anger that terrorism causes—natural consequences of targeting the uninvolved in order to convey a very dramatic message—can lead to an outpouring of cooperation by very large numbers of citizens. This proved true in the case of the World Trade Center bombing, and in the cases of the federal building in Oklahoma City and the Olympics in Atlanta. Then, intelligence and energy alone may be enough—if available in sufficient quantity—to separate the wheat from the chaff and find a manageably short list of suspects. Once that short list is in hand, extremely intensive investigative effort is very likely to produce results.

Without this cooperation, terrorism investigations are likely to fail. That means that maintaining the conditions of that cooperation with every segment of the population that may have relevant knowledge is likely to be crucial.

INVESTIGATIVE SITUATIONS LACKING WILLING WITNESSES

Witnesses who are willing to reveal the existence of a crime, to provide leads to its major suspects, to help in the investigation, and to testify at trial are without doubt the most crucial investigative resource. Without willing witnesses, it may be impossible to learn of certain crimes or to develop a limited list of suspects. Even if these needs can be met, identifying the right defendants and proving guilt at trial will generally require eyewitnesses to the criminal act or the plans leading up to it. When witnesses are unwilling to help—out of fear, indifference, or loyalty to the suspect—investigators have particular difficulty in making and proving a case.

In cases of political violence by members of a disaffected group, both loyalty to the cause and fear of retaliation are likely to discourage witnesses from coming forward. To deal with this, the British in Northern Ireland and the Israeli government allow investigative arrests and prolonged, coercive interrogation. U.S. investigators, not being permitted to use these means, have four principal ways to induce unwilling witnesses to provide the necessary assistance.

First, investigators can offer an otherwise unwilling witness protection or a reward for providing the requested information or assistance. A reward brought the needed information about the

World Trade Center fugitive, Ramzi Yousef. If fear discourages testimony, the witness can either be protected by guards or be given a change of identity. Alternatively, officials may be able to promise to use the witness's information without revealing his identity, by using it only to obtain a warrant to search or to wiretap, or by introducing an undercover agent to the suspects and then relying on the agent to give needed testimony.

The second method for obtaining the cooperation of unwilling witnesses is coercion. A prosecutor can call the witness before a grand jury and require him or her to testify on pain of civil or criminal contempt. If the prosecutor has charged the witness with another crime, or if he is vulnerable to such charges, the witness can be threatened with more serious consequences if he does not testify. Such steps brought Michael Fortier, an associate of Timothy McVeigh in the Oklahoma City bombing plot, to become a witness for the government.

Third, investigators can deceive an unwilling witness or even one of the suspects into providing the information. As in the plot to bomb the Holland Tunnel involving Sheik Abdel-Rahman, an informant can elicit the necessary information from the witness or suspect. Electronic surveillance can accomplish the same results.

Finally, if the criminal conduct addressed by the investigation is planned for the future or is an ongoing activity, undercover agents can compensate for the absence of willing witnesses by offering to participate in the activity as victims, customers, or other business associates. In this case, conduct occurring after the introduction of the agents provides the evidence to support the criminal charges. The convictions of conspiracy to bomb the Holland Tunnel and other dramatic sites in New York were based on such evidence of future plans.

DOES INVESTIGATING TERRORISM DIFFER FROM INVESTIGATING ORGANIZED CRIME? If liberal democracies from the United States to Japan to Italy can accept the normal law enforcement constraints even in dealing with organized crime, why has it seemed necessary for many countries to relax these constraints when they are under a sustained terrorist attack? There are, after all, some striking similarities between terrorist and organized crime groups.

Each type of organization does its best to make it extremely difficult for the government to obtain accomplice witnesses, by choosing members carefully, rigorously controlling dissemination of information, and employing ruthless intimidation. Both types of organization make it difficult to obtain victim witnesses. In one case, because the victims are generally either willing participants in a crime, such as buyers of illegal goods or services, or frightened victims of extortion; in the other case, for similar reasons or because the crimes, such as placing a bomb to explode at a later hour, do not easily allow matching the crime with the criminal. In both cases, prosecutors, judges, and lay fact-finders can be subjected to intimidation; being a judge or a prosecutor in an organized crime case in Palermo or Bogotà is hardly safer than being a judge in a terrorist case in Belfast. In both cases, the organization may enjoy equipment and resources far superior to that of the ordinary criminal.

Part of the answer to why it has appeared necessary to change the rules of law enforcement far more in the case of terrorism is found in the fact that terrorism arouses public fears and anger much more than even organized crime. Still, there are also two real differences. The first I have mentioned: the special difficulty of narrowing the list of suspects to a manageable number is compounded in the case of terrorism. Beyond this, the stakes in bringing terrorist activity to a close are often much higher than the stakes in bringing organized crime or ordinary crime to a close. Terrorism often threatens a continuing course of violence and death. Nor are the victims, as in the case of organized crime, likely to be inside participants with some responsibility for the danger they confront. Faced with the threat of continuing random violence, a nation may conclude that stopping the course of terrorist violence is simply more important, and arouses stronger public demands, than catching people who have committed other crimes, even the leaders of organized vice.

THE RISKS OF CHANGING THE RULES
Changing the basic rules of law enforcement, even to combat terrorism, also evokes substantial fears in democratic nations. One source of such fears is obvious. Few want to change the fundamental

relationship of the citizens to the state in a democracy. This is particularly true in the United States where fears of government enforcement have increased dramatically after the Waco and Ruby Ridge sieges.

The second fear is a pragmatic concern. In other democracies, harsh counter-terrorism measures have sometimes dramatically back-fired, resulting in increased violence, additional recruitment to the terrorist cause, and reduced willingness to assist the government. For example, in Northern Ireland policies allowing widespread war-rantless searches of citizen houses led to increased terrorist group recruitment, especially where the searches were accompanied by excessive use of force by security personnel and extensive destruc-tion of citizen property. Relaxed arrest policies in Northern Ireland and Israel have at times poured kerosene on the fire of terrorist violence, increasing opposition to the government and expanding the scope of the conflict.

These risks are compounded by the possibility that the society will become harshly discriminatory, by application of different sets of rules to different groups. Even if security practices are changed to apply equally to all "suspect" groups, enforcement will often be selective. For example, if some members of ethnic group "A" are involved in a separatist terrorist campaign, the weight of the revised security policy is likely to affect all members of that group. Their houses will be the ones searched. Their members will be the ones arrested or interned. A taste of this problem occurred in the United States during the Gulf War in 1990 and 1991, when many Arab-Americans began to complain of enhanced surveillance that contin-ues years later. Such increased security attention to a particular group is often accompanied by increased suspicion and hostility from citizens. And once the government is viewed as a partisan force in the conflict, rather than as a neutral enforcer of the laws, the spiral of violence is likely to increase along with terrorist recruitment of aggrieved individuals.

No alteration of law enforcement practices is more dangerous, in this regard, than changes in the rules regarding the use of deadly force by government agents.

The Use of Deadly Force

The most serious problems of altered law enforcement policies come in the area of the use of deadly force. In most Western countries, as in the United States, the use of deadly force is strictly regulated. It can be used when necessary to effect the arrest of an armed and dangerous criminal after warning. It can also be used in self-defense or to save the lives of others. These rules contrast with the far looser rules for military engagements between armed forces, which allow the use of deadly force unless the opponent is disarmed or has surrendered. Thus, if the police can safely put even an armed terrorist under arrest, there is no right to shoot; in contrast, there is no obligation to try to capture an armed enemy soldier who has not surrendered.

These rules are widely acknowledged. They are the rules generally followed by the FBI in the United States. Members of the British armed forces have been provided a "Yellow Card" that specifies rules for the use of deadly force in Northern Ireland. The card indicates that military forces must use firearms only as a last resort, provide a challenge before opening fire (such as shouting, "Army! Stop or I fire!"), fire only aimed shots, and fire no more rounds than necessary.

We now know that both Spain and Israel secretly authorized their intelligence agents to assassinate terrorists living abroad, where they could not be arrested and tried. Assassination abroad by any U.S. official is a step that is explicitly forbidden by Presidential Executive Order 12333. We rely on extradition followed by trial or, occasionally, seizures abroad followed by trial as Chapter 4 explained. But whatever one thinks of assassination of murderers who cannot be brought to trial—and it is a very questionable national security practice—there is something far worse about killing suspects who could readily be brought to trial in your own country. That is what has happened on several recent occasions in countries with long democratic traditions.

DEADLY FORCE POLICY

The substantial changes that take place in confronting terrorists occur at the level of implementation, not policy. Examples are uncomfortably ready at hand. Britain asked John Stalker, the deputy chief counsel for Manchester, England, to investigate a series of highly controversial shootings of suspected IRA personnel by the Northern Irish security forces (the Royal Ulster Constabulary, or RUC) in 1982. Six people had been killed in three separate incidents under circumstances suggesting that they could safely have been arrested. Stalker was called in after the officers had been acquitted of murder on the ground, the judge said, that a court can not use a jeweler's scale to measure the reasonableness of Security Force actions in such a case.

Stalker's investigation, staffed by five detectives from Manchester, was exhaustive, involving approximately five hundred interviews. It revealed many questions about the accounts that had been given of the shooting. Shortly before the shooting occurred, three police officers had been killed. An informer gave the Royal Ulster Constabulary the names of IRA personnel allegedly involved in the killing of the police and, within six weeks, four of those named had been killed by the RUC. Stalker concluded that prosecution was warranted.

The British faced similar events in 1988 with the shooting in Gibraltar of three IRA personnel, who were thought to be planning a bombing of British troops in Gibraltar, having carried out similar attacks in Germany and the Netherlands. The shootings were by seven members of the Special Air Service (SAS), the British government's elite anti-terrorist commando unit.

The security forces in Northern Ireland had observed that three well-known IRA personnel had left Belfast and, therefore, faxed their photographs to a variety of European governments. The Spanish police saw the three, noticed them, notified Britain, and kept the three under surveillance. Meanwhile, the SAS was sent to Gibraltar. When the three IRA personnel came to Gibraltar and parked their car near where British soldiers march, the SAS fired, apparently without warning, and continued to fire until the victims were plainly dead. The IRA personnel were unarmed, and there were no explosives in that car, although Spanish investigators later found an IRA vehicle containing explosives nearby in Spain.

The United States has had similar problems on occasion. The Black Panthers and the Symbionese Liberation Army were both subjected to extremely violent and deadly armed attacks. The FBI, in a move that Director Freeh says will not be repeated, approved rules of engagement for its anti-terrorist team (HRT) at Ruby Ridge which specified that agents "could and should" use lethal force without warning against any man seen with a weapon, after a deputy U.S. marshal had been killed by people barricaded in the Idaho home of Randy Weaver. The result was a rifle shot that accidentally killed Weaver's wife. Weaver was a survivalist whose sale of a sawed-off shotgun to a government informer had precipitated an effort to arrest him; his resistance resulted in a standoff that had already led to the death of his teenage son.

Current Department of Justice rules require imminent, or at least plain, danger to life before deadly force may be used. (A requirement of "imminence" may be too cautious in one case. The Supreme Court has held that deadly force may be used if necessary to arrest a suspect who is armed and dangerous and will otherwise escape, because of the danger to life he will later pose. Under similar reasoning, deadly force might well be appropriate to free hostages whose lives are plainly threatened, although not immediately.)

Shoot-to-kill policies are particularly dangerous because they may easily lead to blatant assassination. This slippery slope is illustrated by events in Israel in 1984, when four Arabs from the Gaza Strip seized Bus 300 in southern Israel. A paratrooper unit stormed the hijacked bus, killing two of the hijackers and liberating the hostages. Two other hijackers were led off the bus, but they were killed soon after by agents of Shin Bet, Israel's internal intelligence unit. This was in plain violation of Israeli law, an act of murder.

THE "COVER-UP" THAT FOLLOWS
Rarely have the rules of engagement been openly changed as they were for the FBI siege at Ruby Ridge. There has sometimes been an implicit understanding that "shoot to kill" is permissible, or there has simply been a deep unwillingness of governmental authorities to

prosecute those who are fighting terrorists. So cover-up seems to be a natural attendant to such events.

It appears to have happened in Britain. Stalker submitted an interim report recommending prosecution of those responsible for the killings of IRA personnel in Northern Ireland. The British government then removed him from his post, alleging that he had ties to a Manchester criminal. These allegations were later proven to be utterly false. The investigation begun by Stalker was subsequently completed but not released. In January 1988, the British attorney general, Patrick Mayhew, stated that he had decided not to prosecute the RUC personnel in the national interest, although he acknowledged that there was some evidence of a cover-up in the case.[4] Then again, after the Gibraltar shootings, British Prime Minister Margaret Thatcher indicated that there would be no investigation except for a coroner's jury to determine if the shootings constituted justifiable homicide. The coroner's jury duly found the killings justified.

Nor has the United States been free of this problem. The Department of Justice investigation of what took place at Ruby Ridge was, in the words of FBI Director Freeh, "a flawed investigation," leading later to a U.S. government settlement with the Weaver family by paying $3.1 million and a renewed investigation by both the administration and Congress.

The most dramatic cover-up was the sequel to the killing of the two Arab terrorists by Israeli intelligence in 1984. The government of Israel first took steps to censor any press report that might conflict with the official account that the two terrorists "died of their wounds on their way to the hospital." When one Israeli newspaper, *Hadashot*, published a picture of the two terrorists as they were led away from the bus and revealed that the minister of defense was conducting an internal inquiry, the government censor ordered the newspaper closed for four days, a ruling that was sustained by the High Court of Justice on the ground that *Hadashot* had not submitted the information prior to publication for the censor's review.

Faced with internal inquiries, Shin Bet proceeded with a strategy of giving false information to cover up its actions. The resulting report of the minister of defense was classified "top secret" in any ovent. But the minister of justice also began an inquiry. Shin Bet's successful deceptions in that inquiry led the minister of justice to recommend that the chief of paratroopers, who was not responsible for the killings, be tried for maltreatment of the prisoners and that members of Shin Bet only be brought before an internal disciplinary board and not investigated for matters related to the killings. Fortunately, the chief of paratroopers was cleared at his trial, but on the basis of the false evidence Shin Bet furnished, all members of Shin Bet were also "cleared," despite incontrovertible evidence that they were guilty of murder.

In September 1985, the prime minister and the attorney general were told the truth about Shin Bet's role in the affair by three senior officials of Shin Bet. The prime minister was sufficiently irritated with the messengers who brought that information to want them dismissed, but the attorney general insisted on starting a criminal investigation. Now his staff refused to deal with the representatives of Shin Bet who had earlier deceived them. The effort of the attorney general was met with angry opposition by the entire political leadership of Israel—the prime minister from the Labor Party; the deputy prime minister, the leader of the Likud party; and senior members of their coalition cabinet—all of whom felt that national security precluded any criminal investigation. As an appointed civil servant, the attorney general did not have the power to continue the investigation, but he refused to stop. For the first time in Israel's history an attorney general was then dismissed from office, on June 1, 1986.

On June 25, 1986, two years and two months after the assassinations, the president of Israel acted on the recommendation of Israel's cabinet and pardoned the four top members of Shin Bet for anything they may have done in connection with this affair. In doing so, he issued a statement reminding Israel of everything it owed to the secret activities of Shin Bet in protecting it from dangerous terrorist enemies. The dismissal was simply a small payment on that debt. The pardon was challenged in the High Court of Justice on the grounds that there was no power to pardon before the facts had been determined at a trial. In a divided opinion, the Supreme Court sustained the pardon, although expressing considerable discomfort with the extent to which the Court was forced to swallow a plain violation of the law.

Dealing with the Problems of Intimidation

Witnesses are far more easily subjected to intimidation than are fact-finders—judges or prosecutors. That is true in an ordinary criminal trial in the Bronx, in Guatemala City, Guatemala, and in Palermo, Italy. It is particularly true in cases with suspects who are members of politically violent groups.

Allowing a terrorist suspect to identify the witnesses against him, particularly if they are former accomplices, subjects the witnesses to risks that many will not accept. On the other hand, the unusually tempting incentives (e.g., immunity from prosecution) the government openly offers to witnesses in the most serious of cases in the United States (and which are available in less dramatic forms in other countries) make the right of the defendant to challenge the testimony of prosecution witnesses essential to a fair determination of the truth. For this reason, among others, a right of confrontation is guaranteed by the Sixth Amendment of the United States Constitution, with the narrow and rare exception of cases where the government can prove the witness has been threatened by the defendant.[5]

There are, nevertheless, steps that can be taken to prevent or minimize intimidation. A witness can be protected by police guards during the trial. After the trial, the witness may be hidden somewhere if the country is large enough. The U.S. Witness Protection Program changes the identity and location of between 150 and 300 witnesses each year. Still, this effort is extremely expensive and difficult. Alternatively, the witness's identity can be kept secret at trial. This is the method used in Colombia in the trial of terrorists or narco-terrorists. The price of the Colombian method is to make impossible a full examination of the witness's likely bias, a matter that only the defendant might know and which he could only identify if he knew who the witness was.

The United States relies on still another method of protecting an informant. The informant's statements may be restricted to a limited

Loan Receipt
Liverpool John Moores University
Learning and Information Services

Bethany Szulc
ID: ID7536
Date: 30/04/2007   Time: 11:46

nt.
nt. Gus
e 31111011284254 Loan Type: 1 Day Loan
ate. 01/05/2007   Due Time: 23:59

Fines will be charged on late returns.
Please retain receipt in case of dispute.

use—not as testimony at trial but, for example, only to justify a search or an electronic surveillance, or to improve the prospects of an interrogation. The informant's name need not be given in the affidavit for a search or wiretap warrant which is later made public; it certainly need not be revealed during the course of questioning of a defendant or the pursuit of other leads by the police. Thus, where harm to a witness is feared in the United States, the only evidence presented at trial—the only evidence which the defendant ought to be able to confront—is typically the evidence given by the law enforcement officer as to what was seen or heard during the search or wiretap.

If the incentives to testify can be made great enough for accomplices of the defendant, testimony may be available even if the witness is not protected by anonymity, hiding, or guards. The Italians, departing from a long civil law tradition, supplemented witness protection by creating incentives powerful enough to overcome the threat of retaliation at the hands of the terrorist Red Brigades—by substantially increasing sentences and accompanying the increased punishment with provisions for large reductions in sentence for those who cooperated against their former associates. This is also a major pattern in persuading witnesses in the United States to testify.

FACT-FINDERS

Western European countries have taken cautious steps to eliminate these risks of intimidation. Germany centralized the prosecution and adjudication functions in the case of terrorism, providing special protection for those responsible. For terrorist trials, France eliminated the participation of a majority of lay individuals who act as fact-finders in felony trials, substituting a panel of judges, all but one of whom is anonymous. More dramatically, trials of narco-terrorists and other terrorists in Colombia take place before a single judge whose identity is carefully hidden.

Closest to the U.S. common law tradition is the situation of Great Britain in Northern Ireland. The British "Diplock Courts" are perhaps the most famous of the special anti-terrorism courts in operation. Lord Diplock headed a Commission to evaluate the operation of the Northern Ireland justice system when opposition to internment without judicial trial had led the government to seek alternative ways of processing court cases involving paramilitaries. He concluded that intimidation of jurors by the defendants and their colleagues and "perverse" verdicts rendered by jurors sympathizing with the cause of the government's opponents made jury trials impractical.

The Diplock Commission recommended implementation of special "Diplock" courts for the trial of specified offenses such as murder, weapons offenses, bombings, and the like. Such courts are presided over by a single judge but without the normal jury. The trials have been public; defendants have had legal representation and could cross-examine witnesses against them. The standard for conviction has remained guilt beyond a reasonable doubt. Defendants have an unfettered right to appeal if found guilty. Judges are required to provide a written opinion regarding their views of the law and the facts of the case when rendering a verdict. Their reasoning can be challenged on appeal.

Britain's attorney general is empowered to decide, at the request of defense counsel, if specific cases involving scheduled offenses should be "certified out" as not being political in nature. Cases that are "certified out" revert back to the regular jury trial courts. In 1995, the attorney general approved 932 of 1,234 applications for removal from Diplock Court. In that year 418 people were tried for scheduled offenses in Diplock Court and 395 were convicted (360 of these pleaded guilty). Of the 58 defendants who pleaded not guilty, 23 (40 percent) were found not guilty at trial.[6]

These uses of special courts have been careful and their purpose, avoiding intimidation of fact-finders, is important. But special courts always create special fears because the motivation for special courts has not always been merely to deal with intimidation. Secret courts instituted by the military to further its purposes have been used in Guatemala, Argentina, Chile, and elsewhere. The purpose was less to deal with threats than to ensure that the fact-finders would be sympathetic to the views of the government.

Nothing like special courts has been proposed for the United States, nor would any such proposal be consistent with the right of jury trial guaranteed by the Sixth Amendment of the Constitution. Steps may be taken to protect the anonymity of the jury, but such steps are limited by a parallel judicial concern for the message, and the bias, that comes when the fact-finder is in effect told that the defendant may be a danger to the jury. The closest apparent parallel to a special court in the United States—the creation of a special court for foreign intelligence, charged with issuing warrants for searches or electronic surveillance against agents of foreign powers engaged in international terrorism—has nothing to do with fears of intimidation.

Facilitating Confessions and Searches

Two crucial ways of dealing with a scarcity of willing witnesses are an increased reliance on confessions and wider use of searches and electronic surveillance.

CONFESSIONS

In an effort to compensate for witnesses who might not survive confrontation with the defendant at trial, British law enforcement in Northern Ireland turned to increased reliance on the defendant's confession in place of other evidence. One study showed that confessions occurred in 86 percent of the cases examined and that only 30 percent of these cases had significant additional supporting evidence (such as an eyewitness identification or forensic evidence).

Before the passage of the 1974 anti-terrorist legislation in Great Britain, confessions were only admissible in court if they were considered "voluntary." Thereafter, however, a suspected terrorist's confession, voluntary or involuntary, was admissible as long it was not the product of torture or degrading or inhuman treatment. After some legal dispute, it was accepted that any use or threat of force would render a confession inadmissible under this standard, although whether force was used or threatened was, not surprisingly, subject to vigorous contention in most cases. In addition, judges retained the discretionary power to exclude a confession if it would be unjust to allow its use, although this power has not been used to restore the old "voluntariness" standard through the back door. Interrogation without charge could continue for forty-eight hours. In serious cases, the interrogation could be prolonged for another five days, or seven days in all, through application to the home secretary (for Great Britain) or the Northern Ireland secretary.

Following the 1979 report of the Bennett Committee of Inquiry into Police Interrogation Procedures in Northern Ireland, which investigated reports of abuse by police during interrogation, internal guidelines were issued to safeguard prisoners' well-being during the interrogation. Prisoners were not to be physically attacked, threatened, or abused with obscenities or insulting language. They would be allowed access to their solicitors and could notify a relative, although both could be denied for forty-eight hours if the police feared a "tip-off." In practice, most prisoners did not have the benefit of a solicitor. They would be examined by a doctor to make sure they were not abused. They would not be interrogated during mealtimes or after midnight except when necessary to prevent an imminent terrorist attack. They were to be given a written sheet explaining their rights, and detectives were required to identify themselves by name or number to facilitate complaints of ill-treatment and resulting disciplinary procedures. However, suspects were rarely given a sheet to keep, and only a minority of detectives divulged their names or numbers, presumably from fears of complaints of ill-treatment or reprisals by terrorists. Physical violence was apparently used rarely after the Bennett Committee's recommendations were implemented.

In practice, the police in Northern Ireland and Great Britain have used interrogation not only for obtaining confessions but also for obtaining routine intelligence on persons and communities who are sympathetic to the IRA or Protestant paramilitary bands. Both uses of interrogation have been highly effective in capturing and punishing terrorists.

U.S. Supreme Court decisions under the Fourth, Fifth, and Sixth Amendments to the United States Constitution preclude prolonged interrogation, in the absence of a lawyer, in an effort to obtain a confession.' Any use of physical force or threat would be even more clearly unconstitutional. Federal prosecutors can, however, induce confessions or assistance against co-conspirators by threatening to seek very severe sentences unless the suspect confesses or provides the needed information.[8] This form of pressure has proved adequate to bring confessions in a long string of espionage cases. The different, less-mercenary motivations of terrorists may make the prospects less reassuring, although the technique worked with co-conspirator Michael Fortier in the Oklahoma City bombing case.

SEARCH AND ELECTRONIC SURVEILLANCE

In response to terrorism in Northern Ireland, amendments in 1987 to the Emergency Provisions Act of Northern Ireland authorized police and army personnel to conduct searches without warrants, using a standard of "reasonable suspicion" that was less than the "probable cause" required by the Fourth Amendment to the U.S. Constitution. The 1987 British standard was intended to add some basis for judicial review; prior to that time, no standard for warrantless searches was set out in the legislation. The security forces need higher approval only for a search of a dwelling.

In some years the Northern Irish Security Forces have conducted more than one hundred thousand house searches, discovering thousands of weapons and tons of explosives. The Republic of Ireland has also used the search power extensively. In 1987, after the freighter *Eksund* was seized off the coast of France with a hundred and fifty tons of weaponry destined for the IRA, much of it very sophisticated, Ireland feared that it might be the subject of attack. It reacted by conducting searches of over fifty thousand houses in less than one month, using seven thousand soldiers and police, but little was found.

The benefits of extensive searches have been considerable in Northern Ireland. Close to ten thousand firearms and almost a hundred tons of explosives were seized during the 1970s and 1980s, and the operations of paramilitaries were made far more difficult. But there was a heavy cost; the wholesale searches turned moderates against the government and traumatized the young, leading to increased recruitment by the IRA.

Following a pattern that is special to the United States, Congress in 1994 extended the Foreign Intelligence Surveillance Act to cover searches as well as electronic surveillance where what was involved was international terrorism carried out by an agent of a foreign power. These powers are not to be invoked for law enforcement purposes, but for intelligence needed by policymakers or for prevention. The attorney general may apply to the Foreign Intelligence Surveillance Court, a group of judges specially selected for this purpose by the Chief Justice of the United States, for approval of "a physical search in the United States of the premises, property, information, or material of . . . an agent of a foreign power for the purpose of collecting foreign intelligence information," which includes information about international terrorism.

These requirements are, in practice, considerably easier to satisfy than a traditional law enforcement requirement of showing that a search would probably reveal evidence that the individual whose property is searched was involved in a crime. So long as the purpose was intelligence-gathering, however, the information can be used at trial.

If the application is approved, it must be carried out in conformity with various protective provisions imposed by the court, but then a search may be conducted at any point within as many as forty-five days; the period may also be extended, although it is already far in excess of what would be permitted for an ordinary search. Notice of the search must be given only to a U.S. citizen or resident alien, and then only when the attorney general has determined that there is no national security interest in continuing to maintain secrecy.

The extension of the Foreign Intelligence Surveillance Act is a substitute for the executive power to conduct searches for intelligence purposes under similar circumstances that has long been claimed by U.S. presidents and attorneys general. Because it, like the electronic surveillance provisions of the Act, is limited to agents of foreign powers, it would not help with the need for domestic intelligence in cases like the bombing in Oklahoma City.

Conclusion

The temptation to depart from familiar judicial proceedings and the established rules with regard to arrest, search, and interrogation is great in the case of terrorism. Other responsible democracies have done so, sometimes openly and sometimes surreptitiously in the form of expanded rules with regard to the use of deadly force and suppressed investigations of the use of excessive force. The open way is far more responsible for a democracy; the latter, surreptitiously, is too similar to the activities of repressive regimes faced with violent or non-violent opposition.

Recent cases in the United States suggest that, with the commitment of sufficient resources, U.S. investigators and prosecutors can resolve cases of terrorism. Against that background, it would be a foolish gamble with deeply respected civil liberties to make changes in the protective practices of decades or centuries. In most cases, the changes would not, moreover, be constitutional. Unless the problems of the United States become far greater and the success of its investigators and prosecutors far less, cases of terrorism should be investigated and tried with the same procedures that we use for trying cases of organized crime and other more familiar criminal matters.

Chapter 8

Domestic Intelligence-
Gathering and Processing
in the United States

Every criminal investigation is an attempt to match what can be learned about a crime with information that can be learned about particular suspects, for purposes of prosecution in court. The way the information can be gathered—the investigative procedures—and the ways it can be used at trial are subject to carefully devised sets of rules.

Intelligence-gathering about a violent group has different purposes: to prevent political violence from occurring and to assist political leaders in responding to it in ways in addition to prosecution. The rules for gathering information and the regulations (systems of classification for keeping national security material secret) for its use may also differ from a criminal investigation. Where the rules for gathering the information are more lenient than the rules for criminal investigations, it is because greater importance is attached to preventing violence from occurring and because, not being targeted toward particular suspects, the need for protection of individual rights may be less.

The primary objective of intelligence-gathering is to deal with future danger, not to punish past crimes. As long as a group committed to political violence is at liberty, it poses a serious danger. This difference in primary purpose creates a difference in what information it is crucial to obtain. Prosecutors seeking conviction may have little interest in all but the first two of the following eight questions that are critical to prevention:

• Who are the members actively engaged in planning to use violence for political purposes?

• What is their motivation?

• Where are they located?

• Who in the population is likely to join the group or provide forms of support needed for its continued operations?

• What is the extent and nature of the support the group is receiving from others outside the country, including another state?

• How does the group handle the problems of remaining clandestine and yet carrying out political violence? What is its *modus operandi*?

• What type of attacks is the group capable of?

• What is the strategy behind their planning?

These questions assume that the intelligence-gathering unit—for terrorism in the United States it is the counterintelligence division of the FBI—already knows that there is a threat and can identify, at least crudely, who might be involved. Intelligence-gathering can begin even earlier, scanning the horizon for potential threats. The intelligence agency may look for suspicious signs of preparation such as unusual purchases of explosives, or the arrival in the country of people like Ramzi Yousef, the experienced terrorist who took part in the World Trade Center bombing. Intelligence-gathering, at this earliest stage, might be focused on any suspicious activity around unusually attractive targets, whether a visiting head of state or a nuclear facility. In both cases, efforts would be made to scan or patrol the environment carefully to identify those who might otherwise never be suspected.

Midway between such a "patrol" and knowing about at least the existence of a violent group lies intelligence-gathering focused on individuals or groups that are more likely than others to embark on a course of political violence. Information may have come from abroad. For example, the United States had such information about Sheik Abdel-Rahman from friendly intelligence sources abroad. It may come in the form of a tip from a local informant. Or it might come from observing a social setting in which the necessity of violence for political purposes is preached and taken seriously. That would include, for example, the sermons of Sheik Abdel-Rahman or some of the activities of those associated with right-wing militias in the United States.

The Sources of Intelligence about a Partially Identified Group

Techniques for gathering information about a terrorist group are the same whatever the purposes, whether prevention or prosecution. The differences come in three places. There may be a greater effort to protect the sources and methods involved in intelligence-gathering, so that they can continue to play an important role in prevention. There may be a far more sophisticated effort to bring together bits and pieces of information from many sources and to draw conclusions. Finally, the rules may be looser in intelligence-gathering.

Since terrorism is a form of communication to larger publics, the terrorists themselves are likely to provide hints as to who was involved, perhaps claiming credit for what they have done. Even the fact that the Oklahoma City bombing took place on the second anniversary of the fire at Waco, Texas was a very helpful start. Where the organization has a highly developed philosophy—a worldview to which it hopes to hold its members and that it uses to recruit new support—its writings and proclamations may provide an insight into its likely targets, the groups within which it is likely to find support, and its potential for growth.

The difficulty lies in getting beyond that. A few people may know the answers to the most critical of the questions about a group responsible for political violence. Those individuals are likely to be present or recent members of that terrorist group or organization. An insider furnishing the information on such a "wholesale" basis may have been "turned" by various legal inducements such as plea bargaining or an offer of reward. That was the pattern in the case against Sheik Abdel-Rahman for conspiracy to bomb the Holland Tunnel and the trial of the Oklahoma City bombing. The Israelis and the British, among others, have also used coercive interrogation of suspects and prolonged detention, employing techniques forbidden in the United States. Israeli intelligence claimed that this was crucial to rounding up most of the group that bombed buses in Tel Aviv and Jerusalem in August 1995. Access to inside information could also be obtained by deceiving the insider into placing trust in someone who is secretly reporting to the government or by putting pressure on someone, perhaps a family member, friend, or lover, in whom the terrorist has confided, as was done in the Oklahoma City case.

The terrorist group will try to deny this greatest source of information, an inside informant, to the government. It will often be very selective in its membership, requiring a long history of association with related causes, although the cost of this is to limit sharply the growth of the organization. As a rite of initiation or test of loyalty, the group may require new members to commit violent crimes in which police or government intelligence agencies would be legally forbidden to participate. It can organize itself in a cell structure that limits sharply the amount that any single member knows. It can take severe reprisals against informants or, if they are protected, against their families. It can maintain an above-ground front organization to provide support and encourage sympathy for the hard-core underground, whose activities would be largely unknown to the front members.

In most cases, therefore, the investigators cannot count on finding and enjoying the cooperation of someone with all the knowledge the investigators need. They are more likely to have access to isolated bits of information, obtained from a variety of sources. Citizens may have seen suspicious people or objects near the scene of a bombing or kidnapping or assassination, as in the case of an early effort by the Unabomber, Theodore Kaczynski. The police or a security video camera may have observed a car of a particular type and license plate parked nearby. The pamphlets left behind can provide some clues. The crime scene may contain traces, such as the type of explosive used, or a fingerprint, or the identification number of a rented vehicle, as in the World Trade Center and Oklahoma City cases.

Terrorist organizations, like any other clandestine group that engages in crime, will do their very best to hide physical evidence bearing on these eight questions. But that is never entirely possible. Physical evidence or observations may be left at the scene of a kidnapping or bombing. Such evidence helped identify those responsible for the destruction over Lockerbie, Scotland, of Pan Am Flight 103, for the bombing of the World Trade Center, and for the bombing of the Oklahoma City federal building. In each case, the effort required of investigators was massive, but the results were worth the effort.

Other evidence may come from physical searches based on reason to believe that a place has been used to plan or carry out terrorist activities. Aggressive patrol by the police in the vicinity of recent or suspected terrorist activity, including the demand for identification of passers-by (if the law permits), may produce additional bits of useful information. Another form of patrol, less limited by location, can be an undercover offer to sell equipment or material that the terrorists are likely to need and which, perhaps because of legal prohibitions, they find difficult to obtain. Many types of potentially relevant information may have been found in records that are public or at least available to investigators. Money flows and other financial transactions can be traced through bank records. Records are often kept of the sale of chemicals and some explosives. There are records of thefts of explosives and, as in the Oklahoma City case, of weapons. In many countries, certain forms of arms must be registered and their serial numbers recorded. Official records of travel into and out of the country, airline passenger manifests, or even rental records can be helpful. Without more evidence, no such record is incriminating. But, if it can be combined with other information, it may produce a very revealing pattern.

Since the problem is often to match people with events, fragments of history also provide clues. For some individuals, clandestine violence has been preceded by a record of less violent, politically radical activities, or a close association with others who are already known to be terrorists. Timothy McVeigh and Terry Nichols, later convicted of the Oklahoma City bombing, together robbed a gun dealer. Several defendants in the bombing of the World Trade Center in New York were believed to have earlier plotted to kill Rabbi Meir

Kahane. A history of suspected terrorism followed by a disappearance from view suggests that the person may belong to, or may have joined, an underground terrorist group. Observations of people with whom suspects associate and where they congregate add other names, with their own histories. This was critical in the World Trade Center case.

For those creating useful intelligence, the goal is often to be able to combine a large number of seemingly unrelated pieces of information and find within them a revealing pattern. Today, this goal is accomplished through the use of powerful computers. Such computers may contain voluminous arrest and conviction records, records of fugitives and relevant identifying data, lists of material objects that have been seized, etc. But modern computer analysis can go much further. It can spot linkages among the thousands and thousands of individual pieces of information in the database.

Germany pioneered the use of computers in this field. The German federal police agency, the BKA, designed a special computer-based cross-reference system (called "PIOS") as early as 1976, in direct response to terrorism. The BKA systematically put into its database every possible clue: every address found in a suspect's possession, the phone numbers and names of each visitor to a suspect in prison, information relating to every object found at the scene of a terrorist incident or at a place where terrorists resided, all known contacts among suspects, all movements, etc. Two apparently unrelated individuals could be shown to be extremely likely to belong to the same terrorist group by showing an overlap in the information about them which was too complete to be coincidental. New directions for further investigation were often suggested.

The technique is the familiar one of "grid" analysis, but made far more powerful by the use of computers. It may be known that "A" belongs to a particular terrorist group "G," and lives in a particular residence "D." "B" may be known to belong to a different group, "H," that uses a known safe house "E." If an agent in Omaha now discovers that "C" visits the safe house "E" and stores that information in the computer, and another agent in Miami sees "C" at the residence "D" and stores that information, new investigative leads will be made apparent by the computer program: it gives reason to suspect that the two organizations may be related and that "A" and "B" may be cooperating with each other.

In the same way, an individual could be tied to a terrorist event. Indeed, the German BKA learned to use the capacity in "real time" for dealing with ongoing crises. Massive amounts of seemingly trivial information about a major terrorist event, such as a high-level kidnapping, could be used in the task of finding out who was involved and where they might be holding the hostage. Using this technique, the BKA came within a hair's breadth of solving one of its most famous terrorist kidnappings, that of Dr. Hanns-Martin Schleyer.

The Germans, prodded by the needs of dealing with violent domestic groups such as the Red Army Faction, also led in designing computer technologies to assist in locating fugitives. With the help of the vast database of all information that might have any pertinence, collected and indexed, among other ways, under the name of particular suspected terrorists, the police can design strategies making use of levels of detail that the suspect is unlikely to consider in developing his own strategies for evasion of arrest. For example, if the computer supplied information that the suspect always telephoned his mother on her birthday, a call to her on that day could be traced or tapped. Knowledge that he was an enthusiast about a certain soccer team might lead investigators to travel to all the team's matches.

A third important capacity of computer processing is simply the ability of the computer to review vast collections of records in a very short time, selecting those that are of particular interest to the investigators, or simply to identify, for further attention, statistical "outliers" within any mass of quantified data. The technique is a form of electronic patrol. For example, the BKA has used its capacities to engage in "computer-based examination of a large circle of persons through certain data and characteristics that are typical for a narrowly defined group of suspicious persons." The German police believe that a typical terrorist characteristic is to pay rent or electric utility bills in cash. A review of all files of bills paid in cash, furnished by the electric company, creates a smaller sub-category which can then be correlated with other characteristics, such as age, occupation, or, more questionably, political affiliations. The remaining names may be the basis for more intensive investigation.

The FBI has now refined and expanded upon the capacities pioneered by the German police. In 1996, David Burnham described the result in *Above The Law*:

> The Justice Department's new-age investigative entity, actually a conglomeration of many different technologies, has in a strange way begun to assume some of the basic properties of a living and growing organism. The system boasts a kind of reproductive process, a semi-secret facility specifically established to beget a vast range of sophisticated electronic surveillance devices. It possesses a gigantic maw that uses these devices and other kinds of computerized collection systems to ingest, swiftly and cheaply, hundreds of millions of pieces of information about both the general public and the much smaller number of individuals actually suspected of committing criminal acts.
>
> The entity also is beginning to develop something close to a brain in the form of an expanding stable of advanced computers specifically designed to draw investigative inferences from the organized examination of all the data that the Justice Department and its component agencies are collecting.[1]

The Rules for Gathering Intelligence about Violent U.S. Groups

Two types of rules are important with regard to intelligence-gathering: the rules regulating on what basis an organization can be monitored at all (i.e., an investigation initiated), which are discussed in the next section; and the rules regulating the techniques available for gathering information that citizens would like to keep private. In either of these categories for intelligence-gathering about domestic groups that may be violent, the rules may be the same as for investigating ordinary crimes, or they may be special to terrorist investigations. To a large extent, the rules in the United States are no different for intelligence-gathering than from the rules for criminal investigations, despite the argument accepted in other countries that prevention of terrorism justifies more extreme measures than punishment of crime.

DEFINING THE AREAS WHERE SPECIAL RULES APPLY

Where the rules do differ in any Western democracy, it is essential to define the category of matters to which more permissive "intelligence" rules apply. The definition can be created in terms of the purpose of the enterprise—prevention or aiding policymakers as opposed to prosecution. It can be made in terms of the activity being investigated: for example, is it espionage or terrorism? It can depend upon the more remote purposes of the organization being monitored: for example, does it aim to overthrow the present governmental structure? Finally, the distinction may turn on the citizenship of the participants in political violence, or the nature of their relationship to foreign governments.

In the United States, special intelligence-gathering powers can only be used against agents of foreign countries or parties who are engaged in espionage or international terrorism. The conditions for intelligence-gathering are different in Germany, Great Britain, and other Western democracies. The German intelligence agency, the Bureau for the Protection of the Constitution (BfV), is authorized to collect and evaluate information on individuals and groups concerning "efforts" or activities aimed against "the free democratic constitutional order." It has considerable discretion in determining when the standard is met. For example, in 1996 some argued that the standard authorized gathering intelligence on the German branch of the U.S.-based Church of Scientology.

Officially, the BfV distinguishes between "extremists" and merely "radical" activities, with only the former subject to intelligence monitoring. Whatever nuances of the distinction, the intent is plainly to include the ability to investigate organizations that have nothing to do with international terrorism or foreign sponsorship. This is reflected in the organization of Germany's BfV, which contains three separate sections for monitoring and combating terrorism. Section Two deals with domestic right-wing terrorism and extremist movements. Section Six deals with international and foreign terrorism.

And Section Seven is responsible for domestic left-wing terrorism and extremist movements. The BfV's analogs at the state (*lander*) level have taken similar language very far. The Berlin intelligence office spied on, monitored, and wire-tapped the private conversations of certain Social Democratic and Green Party members of the Berlin Parliament, as well as several prominent attorneys and journalists over a several-year period.

THE RULES REGARDING THE USE OF PARTICULAR TECHNIQUES TO GATHER
INTELLIGENCE ABOUT CITIZENS SUSPECTED OF TERRORISM

There is only one source of special investigative power for intelligence-gathering about American citizens within the United States. The Foreign Intelligence Surveillance Act defines those "foreign intelligence" cases in which electronic surveillance and, since 1994, physical search are available under special criteria. These render an American citizen subject to electronic surveillance or a physical search if he engages in, assists, or agrees to assist in "international terrorism" as an agent of a foreign power. The statute states explicitly "that no United States person may be considered . . . an agent of a foreign power solely on the basis of activities protected by the First Amendment to the Constitution of the United States." In practice, these requirements are far easier to satisfy than the normal probable-cause requirements for a wire tap or a search in a criminal case.

This is the only exception to the familiar powers the government already enjoys in the law enforcement area, and to the equally familiar rules that surround those powers: a search in a private place or an electronic surveillance of a place or telephone cannot take place without explicit probable cause to believe that evidence of a crime will be found. Interrogation must comply with the familiar *Miranda* rules requiring warnings and access to an attorney, and must not violate the suspect's rights to counsel after the formal criminal process has begun. An undercover offer to engage in crime that entices someone not predisposed to that type of crime is "entrapment," and a resulting conviction will be set aside.

As to a number of other very powerful information-gathering devices, there is practically no regulation in the United States. Investigators may interview any willing witness, and may let the unwilling know that his reluctance to talk will increase their suspicion. Normal physical surveillance of people or premises requires no special factual basis or predicate if the investigation is otherwise proper. The same is true of turning an insider into an informant or infiltrating a government agent into a group or offering rewards for information, including a substantially reduced sentence for someone guilty of another offense. Any property or records that are publicly available may be viewed and analyzed; the same is true of any private places or records that are made available by someone properly possessing them. There is no limit on when or how U.S. agencies may seek evidence from other foreign or domestic governmental units engaged in similar investigations.

Finally, a grand jury subpoena may be used, almost without any explanation beyond that the grand jury is involved in a *bona fide* investigation of a crime, to obtain documents, testimony, hair or voice samples, or participation in a line-up. The suspect cannot be required to give testimony that incriminates himself unless he is first given immunity from its use against him, but this Fifth Amendment protection applies only to "testimony" (not records or diaries or such physical evidence as hair, fingerprints, line-ups, etc.) and, if they think it is wise, prosecutors can give immunity and force even testimony.

The United States has not sought significant increases in the powers of its investigators in light of the terrorist bombings of the 1990s. Indeed, as we have seen, the FBI solved each of these crimes quickly using only the powers listed above plus a substantial commitment of manpower. President Clinton's terrorist legislation, passed in 1996, is modest. It increases the ease with which investigators can obtain credit card and other financial records for the purpose of investigating terrorism, and it greatly increases the resources available to federal investigators and the ease with which they can bring together diverse sources of information in the hands of various agencies.

But the changes in legal investigative powers are minor, especially compared to the nearly universal practices in other Western democracies. Britain, Germany, Israel, and many other countries allow intelligence agencies to operate with their own procedures, outside the rules for law enforcement, so long as they are seeking information for policymakers and not evidence for trials. It is revealing to compare the nature of U.S. intelligence-gathering powers over domestic terrorism with those that Great Britain has specially authorized for dealing with problems in Northern Ireland.

A CONTRAST WITH NORTHERN IRELAND

The powers of U.S. investigators to gather intelligence seem very small compared to those enacted by the United Kingdom during the campaign of the Provisional IRA in Northern Ireland, which began in 1969 and has lasted for more than 25 years. The Prevention of Terrorism Acts made it a crime to withhold information about terrorism from police, subject to a defense of duress or other "reasonable excuse." The British have used this statute largely to press acquaintances and family members of suspected terrorists for information, and to induce victims of such crimes as auto theft or car-jacking to report the crime promptly to the police in the hopes of preventing the use of the vehicle in a bombing. (To some extent, the statute has also been used to prosecute those that police thought to be terrorists where the evidence of any other crime was weak or lacking.) Most commentators consider the use to have been relatively effective.

The FBI followed a somewhat similar path in the Oklahoma City investigation, charging Michael Fortier, an acquaintance of the suspects, under ancient and rarely used statutes forbidding "misprision of felony" (concealing evidence of a felony) to induce him to cooperate against McVeigh and Nichols. The tactic was contrary to long traditions in Great Britain and the United States, but the values underlying the tradition are neither strong nor widely supported: the social value of concealing from the police relevant information about another's serious crime is far from clear. Separate issues are, of course, raised by the applicability of such a statute to force investigative journalists or defense attorneys to divulge information, but these issues can be distinguished.

In Great Britain, the anti-terrorist legislation also gave police officers wide authority to search in private places, including homes, in Northern Ireland without a warrant or probable cause. A requirement of "reasonable suspicion" was added only after some years. The record suggests that this practice, which would surely be contrary to the U.S. Fourth Amendment, was effective in discovering large amounts of evidence and confiscating explosives and other firearms. But the record also indicates that it was so offensive to those whose houses were searched that it became a major stimulant to enlistment in the Provisional IRA.

The police in Northern Ireland and Great Britain used coercive interrogation not only for obtaining confessions but also for obtaining routine intelligence from persons and communities they believed were sympathetic to the IRA or Protestant paramilitary bands. Most experts believe this use of interrogation—which would be forbidden in the United States under current rulings of the Supreme Court— was effective in identifying and capturing terrorists, although at a high cost both in civil liberties and in community support.

Ordinary citizens were liable to be arrested and interrogated despite their innocence. In particular, the police regularly used custodial interrogation to obtain information about persons and communities that were not actually suspected of any crimes. Furthermore, many of those in investigative detention were routinely subjected to foul language and insults, often based on their religion or ethnic group. The security forces built up detailed dossiers on every detainee, which were later used to identify suspects and to develop profiles of neighborhoods that were considered terrorist strongholds. The arrest and interrogation power was also used to confirm leads that the police obtained through confidential telephone tips.

The police used custodial interrogation rather than traditional policing (such as gathering physical evidence or questioning suspects at home or on the street) because communities in Northern Ireland were hostile or intimidated, and because officers could not operate freely in neighborhoods dominated by the paramilitaries. Perhaps for this reason, the widespread use of custodial interrogation for intelligence-gathering was confined largely to Northern Ireland. Even there, many believe, its advantages were offset by its effect of stimulating IRA recruitment.

The use of investigative detention has been taken further. In the wake of bombings of buses in Tel Aviv and Jerusalem by suicide bombers during the summer of 1995, Israel quickly increased the powers of its intelligence agency, Shin Bet, to use "moderate physical force" in interrogation. Leaders of Shin Bet have said that the second bombing, in Jerusalem, would have been prevented had they been permitted to use such coercion in interrogation of a prime suspect then in their custody.[2]

The case for coercive interrogation is far weaker in the United States than it has been in the United Kingdom and Israel. The terrorist threat is far less serious and far less sustained. The availability to U.S. investigators of the threats of long prison sentences, reducible only in exchange for cooperation, has proved to be a powerful tool. All three countries also have alternative forms of secret surveillance—by informants or secret government agents or electronic measures—available as partial substitutes for coercion.

The Rules for Initiating an Investigation and the Deep Dilemma about Intelligence Investigations in a Democracy

I have reserved for last the most important and contentious issue with regard to intelligence-gathering in the area of terrorism, and that is its potential chilling effect on free speech. There are identifiable social and political circles that are most likely to inspire and support individuals or groups contemplating political violence. Monitoring those circles of association and stimulating revealing conversations among the participants is a useful strategy of intelligence-gathering. It may be true that looking for terrorists in Sheik Rahman's congregation or among those who attend militia meetings would be like looking for a needle in a haystack of "mere talk." But identifying the right haystack among a field of haystacks can be a sensible way of starting to look for the needle.

The problem is that government monitoring of political and social groups and keeping records of what is said by whom gravely inhibit free discussion and free association—two values whose importance to democracy is reflected in the Bill of Rights. Behind the monitoring is obvious suspicion of serious wrongdoing by the association or its members. No one wants to invite his government to attach that suspicion to him personally as well. The issue is most difficult when the political philosophy of a group includes the necessity of violent action either soon or under a contingency that is quite likely to occur. For purposes of criminal prosecution, the U.S. Supreme Court has protected the right to engage even in such speech, unless the threat of violence is imminent, but it has never questioned the different, although related, right to monitor and gather information.

THE RULES ON THE INITIATION AND SCOPE OF AN INTELLIGENCE INVESTIGATION
In the aftermath of Watergate and revelations of FBI abuses with regard to civil rights leaders and Vietnam War protestors, President Gerald Ford's attorney general, Edward Levi, produced guidelines limiting domestic security investigations by the federal government of groups that are not associated with a foreign power. Amended during the Reagan administration, the guidelines now allow a domestic security/terrorism investigation only when:

the facts or circumstances reasonably indicate that two or more persons are engaged in an enterprise for the purpose of furthering political or social goals wholly or in part through activities that involve force or violence and a violation of the criminal laws of the United States.[3]

The guidelines state that such criminal intelligence investigations differ from the more familiar criminal investigations in that they are not confined to determining who committed an act and establishing the elements of the offense, but may also include efforts to determine "the size and composition of the group involved, its geographic dimensions, its past acts and intended criminal goals, and its capacity for harm." Also, the investigation does not necessarily end with the decision to prosecute. Because "it often requires the fitting together of bits and pieces of information, many meaningless by themselves, to determine whether a pattern of criminal activity exists . . . the investigation is broader and less discriminant than unusual." In such an investigation, "the FBI may use any lawful investigative technique." So, once a domestic security investigation of a group or enterprise is properly initiated, it is proper to gather a great deal of information about its activities, members, and resources over a long period of time. The requirements for initiating such an investigation thus become critically important.

The attorney general's guidelines make clear that the standard of "reasonable indication" necessary to initiate a domestic security investigation is "substantially lower than probable cause." Moreover, the standard is to be determined in light of "the magnitude of the threatened harm." The crucial question remains: to what extent can the FBI investigate groups that advocate violence as a practical necessity for pursuing their political ends?

FBI Director Louis Freeh has explained that the "reasonable indication" standard for opening a criminal intelligence investigation would be satisfied if there were advocacy of violence that would violate the federal criminal statutes, if "the activities of those engaged in the enterprise manifest an apparent ability to carry out violent activity." But the required indications of that last condition are significant: he gives as examples paramilitary organization and training, or the accumulation of explosives.

If the information available to the FBI falls short of the "reasonable indication" standard, something less than an investigation—a "preliminary inquiry"—can be opened under other provisions of the attorney general's guidelines, if the FBI receives information "indicating the possibility of criminal activity" and something more than a cursory check seems appropriate. Such a preliminary inquiry would, the FBI argues, be justified when an individual or a group advocates violence in a context suggesting enough of an ability or intent to carry out violence that there is a risk of harm. Similarly, information that an individual has accumulated explosives would justify either a preliminary inquiry or a lesser step, a "limited checking out of leads."[4]

The guidelines provide that almost any lawful investigative technique may be used in a preliminary inquiry. In addition to collecting and reviewing any publicly available materials, it includes the use of informants or the placing of undercover agents in the organization, if there are "compelling circumstances" and "other investigative means are not likely to be successful." In sum, the attorney general's guidelines allow investigation when "statements advocate criminal activity or indicate an apparent attempt to engage in crime, particularly crimes of violence . . . unless it is apparent, from the circumstances or the context in which the statements are made, that there is no prospect of harm." Quoting a federal Court of Appeals opinion, the director's instructions to the field state that the "FBI always has investigated people who advocate or threaten to commit serious violations of federal law, even if the violations are not imminent; and it always will."

THE INHERENT TENSION BETWEEN INTELLIGENCE INVESTIGATIONS AND POLITICAL FREEDOMS

Whatever the rules, whatever the procedures established, four unavoidable facts create a deep dilemma for democratic values. First, knowing the supporters and potential supporters of a terrorist group is extremely useful in preventing political violence and capturing its perpetrators. Knowing the supporters of those engaged in political violence, a democratic government can prevent them from giving essential support. It can assess the danger of expansion of the violence. It can predict tactics with greater accuracy. It can recognize likely recruits.

Second, political violence is carried out for political ends. Those who support similar ends are more likely than others to be active supporters of groups engaged in political violence. Those who feel deeply enough about that set of issues to become active politically are still more likely to be supporters. It is of course true that only a tiny portion of those with similar views would provide active support for political violence, because of the powerful legal and social inhibitions against committing criminal acts and, most seriously, against committing violent crimes. Still, knowing that someone is politically active on behalf of positions similar to those of a terrorist group tells investigators that, however unlikely it is that the person is himself supporting criminal violence, he is much more likely to be a supporter than are others in the population.

Third, it is therefore logical for investigators—even those who are concerned *only* about violent criminal conduct for political purposes—to want to gather information about those who are actively supporting the same political positions as the terrorist group, although they may be doing so in purely legal and democratic ways. Collecting information on too many people and too many groups may, at some point, be more costly than it is worth. But the costs of storing information and having intelligent access to it are being dramatically reduced because of the expanding powers of computers.

Fourth, and finally, however, the surveillance of groups that are actively opposing governmental policies poses a serious threat to democratic values, even when no intrusive means are used to carry out the surveillance. People have fears, partly rational and partly not, of the response of even democratic administrations to active, legal opposition. They fear the wide discretion of contemporary governments in everything from appointments to arrests and how information about opposition may play into that. They fear that there may be an effort to damage their reputations with private groups that can affect them in other ways. If they do not trust the legality of the government, they may fear petty harassment in the name of law enforcement or even actual physical attacks.

In a 1989 report entitled "The FBI and CISPES," the Select Committee on Intelligence of the United States Senate described the dangers to democratic values in this way:

The American people have the right to disagree with the policies of their government, to support unpopular political causes, and to associate with others in the peaceful expression of those views, without fear of investigation by the FBI or any other government agency. As Justice Lewis Powell wrote in the *Keith* case, "The price of lawful public dissent must not be a dread of subjection to an unchecked surveillance power."

. . . Unjustified investigations of political expression and dissent can have a debilitating effect upon our political system. When people see that this can happen, they become wary of associating with groups that disagree with the government and more wary of what they say and write. The impact is to undermine the effectiveness of popular self-government. If the people are inhibited in expressing their views, a nation's government becomes increasingly divorced from the will of its citizens.[5]

The FBI investigation of the Committee in Solidarity with the People of El Salvador (CISPES) provides a vivid example of the dangers of intelligence investigations. It is also a rare example of an investigation that was reviewed carefully by committees in both Houses of Congress; the results were largely made public. I therefore use this event as an example, although the Senate Intelligence Committee Report of July 1989, the source for all that follows, assures the reader that the case "was an aberration among the thousands of counter-intelligence and counter terrorist investigations the FBI conducts annually" and that "no similar case has come to the Committee's attention, and the Committee's oversight of other FBI activities has found a definite pattern of adherence to established safeguards for Constitutional rights."[6]

A DRAMATIC EXAMPLE

After years of intensive investigation by the FBI, we know the following about CISPES. It was an organization dedicated to public opposition to the policy of the United States of providing military and other support to the government of El Salvador. It was never found to be under any foreign control, including the control of the guerrilla left, the Farabundo Marti National Liberation Front (FMLN) attempting to overthrow the government of El Salvador. It was never found to be secretly funding guerrilla warfare in El Salvador. It never engaged in terrorism within the United States. There may have been individuals associated with CISPES who worked closely with the

Salvadoran FMLN and who provided financial support for its war, although this was never confirmed. No connections of CISPES members to terrorist violence in the United States were ever established.

The FBI investigated CISPES from 1981 to 1985. Attempting to find out what its leadership and membership were doing in each of the locations at which CISPES chapters existed, the FBI used photographic and visual surveillance of rallies and demonstrations (twenty-two field offices), undercover operatives who attended meetings (five offices), informants, interviews of people going to Central America, trash examinations (six field offices), examination of bank records (six offices), study of telephone toll records (fourteen field offices) and the use of a number of quasi-public records involving licenses, credit, employment, utilities, etc. The Senate Select Committee on Intelligence estimated that the main CISPES investigation resulted in retrievable information being added to FBI files on approximately 2375 individuals and 1330 groups. There were also limited investigations of a number of groups whose membership overlapped with CISPES or who seemed to be ideologically similar.

The result was inevitably to discourage some citizens from supporting democratic, political efforts to change U.S. foreign policy in Central America. More broadly, those contemplating active, legal, democratic opposition to government policies, particularly in the area of foreign affairs, are likely to remember that they may be the subject of surveillance and recorded information with unpredictable consequences for their futures and careers.

The Senate Report makes much of the FBI's failure to recognize the unreliability of a single informant, Frank Varelli, whose reports on CISPES provided much of the basis for initiating and then extending the investigation.

There was no effort to check with local police in other parts of the country where Mr. Varelli had studied or worked, to ask other U.S. government agencies whether they had relevant information on him or to follow up on the failure of efforts to find U.S. government files with his fingerprints or military record. . . . No thought was given moreover to polygraphing Mr. Varelli, despite the fact that his description of events leading up to his immigration varied from one account to the next."[7]

The Senate Report makes a variety of other criticisms of how the case was handled, but there is also a deeper, darker problem here. Consider the context of the four-year investigation. The government of the United States was, as a matter of official policy, providing large amounts of military assistance to the government of El Salvador. This was opposed by sizeable segments of the American public attentive to events in Central America. Some portion of these opponents—no one knows what portion—would have favored a victory by the FMLN over the Salvadoran government. Some very small part of that portion who would favor the FMLN would be prepared to furnish funds and aid to it. Some fraction of that portion of the large number opposed to the policy would also be prepared to support violent, politically motivated crimes in the United States.

In retrospect, with the advantage of the FBI investigation and the Intelligence Committee Reports on that investigation, we can tell that CISPES was broadly representative of those opposed to our military support of the government in El Salvador. There was never an adequate reason to believe that as an organization it supported criminal violence or that any significant number of its members or leaders did. Why then was it investigated for four years with significant costs to the vigor of our political processes? Why could a single, lying informant bring a massive intelligence-gathering apparatus into operation and keep it at work on an organization exercising only the most fundamental of democratic liberties?

I have already argued that, if one were looking for those engaged in violent criminal conduct in support of a particular goal, it would be sensible to begin by looking at those who simply support similar views with unusual intensity and energy. But here, when the investigation began, there was no evidence of violent crimes by members of CISPES. There was only passionate political opposition. There was simply a deep suspicion of the patriotism of the opponents of the position taken by our government in El Salvador. The investigators traveled in different groups from the members of CISPES; they did not know CISPES members informally. They acted on a fear of conspiracy by strangers, and a willingness to explain away the incontestible fact that CISPES was broadly populated with people of entirely lawful democratic values as evidence that even people of good will can be duped. It was in this atmosphere that a single informant's seeds of unreliable information could grow so luxuriously.

Suspicion breeds on itself and seeks confirmatory information. CISPES was of course providing political support to the FMLN. Was it not reasonable then to suspect that it was also providing financial support? The Senate Report points out that even as severe a critic of our policies in Central America as former Ambassador to El Salvador Robert White told the FBI that he suspected that CISPES was providing financial support. And if it was providing such support was there not reason to believe that it was receiving direction from the political party it was supporting, the FMLN? On such a flimsy basis, the Department of Justice itself asked for an investigation of this question.

There were bombs set off in Washington protesting our policy in El Salvador. Wouldn't an investigation of the leaders of an organization like CISPES be likely to throw some light on those violent crimes? The barriers set up by rules protecting civil liberties are not very strong. An organization can properly be investigated under the provisions of the Foreign Intelligence Surveillance Act if, on behalf of a foreign state or party, it provides aid to international terrorism, i.e., if it provides financial support to an organization like the FMLN (a "foreign power") which, as part of its war in El Salvador, was certainly committing acts that would have violated the laws of the United States if committed here and were intended "to influence the policy of [the Salvadoran] government by intimidation or coercion." CISPES was readily suspected of providing such aid.

The point is simply this. Management can be improved. Informants like Varelli can be checked more thoroughly. Reviews within the FBI can be more rigorous and frequent. But, when all is said and done, two facts will remain, posing a grave dilemma for democratic values: first, it will make sense, as a pure matter of investigative strategy, to gather information on political supporters of the same cause embraced by those engaged in political violence. And second, in many cases the investigators will find themselves deeply opposed to the viewpoints of those they are investigating and deeply separated by background from an understanding of the views and social structure of the opponents of government policy. Together, these two facts provide fertile ground for conspiracy theories and easy assumptions about the transition from political support to financial support to political violence. Not to gather intelligence is to tie one's hands in a fight against political violence. To gather intelligence is to invite the harms to vital democratic debate that come from known surveillance of political opponents of the administration in power and of the viewpoints it, and perhaps the major opposition parties, represent.

Conclusion

The primary task of domestic intelligence-gathering is prevention of political violence. Its central tool is the careful synthesis of many apparently disparate forms of information. To gather that information, intelligence agencies in other countries have been given a range of special powers, but in the United States investigators must rely on the same powers enjoyed by police agencies with one narrow exception: somewhat relaxed rules for search and electronic surveillance when it can be proved that the target is an agent of a foreign power involved in international terrorism.

A crucial protection for political dissent is the assurance that the government will not monitor private or public meetings of a group sharply criticizing the government. But when such groups urge violence as a response to their criticisms, monitoring their membership and activities may be important to early discovery of extremely dangerous political violence. Drawing this line is the most important step in regulating domestic intelligence-gathering. It is done differently in different democracies but nowhere with more restraint than in the United States. In the end, the limited threat to uninhibited discussion posed by even reasonable efforts to monitor organizations preaching violence is a price worth paying to prevent political violence.

Chapter 9

A Strategy of Common Sense

I began this book with a reminder that a democratic nation wants life, liberty, and unity as the products of its policies for dealing with terrorism, not just physical security. Focusing exclusively on a very popular desire for revenge—treating terrorism as if it were nothing but a common crime—is likely to provide too little liberty and unity to be a sensible policy. Urged on us by Israel's Prime Minister Netanyahu, this policy has not served his country well.

A multiplicity of goals is not the only reason for a sophisticated strategy to deal with terrorism. The opponents who resort to terrorism are trying to affect the politics of a democracy, not simply make war upon it, and they are understood by themselves and their supporters as something different from common criminals and something more than mad. So the targets of our efforts as well as the objectives of our policies are complicated. The result is the need for a rich strategy that cannot be summarized in a single slogan, although the temptation to do that is nearly irresistible for an elected official.

As terrible as were the terrorist attacks on Americans abroad, until 1993 most Americans felt secure against any major political violence at home. Although such events are still rare, the bombings of the World Trade Center and of the federal building in Oklahoma City have demonstrated a vulnerability to political violence within our own borders and by our own citizens. They have also shown that the damage is likely to grow. Each involved a massive explosion in a densely populated area using easily obtained materials. Even the size of those explosions would soon seem ordinary if, as many fear, terrorists can take advantage of the collapse of the Soviet Union to obtain the materials for nuclear weapons. Equally dangerous biological weapons may also be within reach, breaking a long tradition of terrorists using only more familiar and conventional weapons.

The reaction to new fears is often instinctive and angry. But what we need is a strategy that reflects multiple goals and a complicated phenomenon called by a single name, "terrorism." This book has been an effort to describe what such a complicated strategy would be: a strategy that respects law and is concerned for life, liberty, and unity.

The starting point is to recognize that the threat of terrorism cannot be completely eliminated. Violence for political purposes against American citizens and interests will continue. To some, terrorism will continue to look like the best prospect for sharply changing the policies of a very powerful government whose policies are very widely supported by its citizens. Impassioned recruits are available here and abroad; the equipment and knowledge necessary for causing terror is readily at hand. Moreover, in a world where powerful secular states are challenged by fundamentalist religious movements and where new forms of nationalism are bursting free of the forces that suppressed them during the Cold War, there are ample "causes" based on resentments of U.S. policy, whatever it may be. Nor will relatively weak but hostile states give up the opportunity to respond to U.S. power by secret support of violence.

No one knows the scale of these risks. What is clear is that we would be wise to invest in precautions that we deeply hope will never be needed. What would that mean for the United States? To address that question, it is useful to divide the terrorist threat into its traditional component, now expanding to reach targets within our own borders, and the risk of terrorism with nuclear, biological, or chemical weapons ("NBC weapons").

NBC weapons in the hands of sub-state groups may pose the greatest danger to the national security of the United States in the decades following the collapse of Soviet power.[1] For the possibility of use of NBC weapons, however unlikely, we should plan as we have for unlikely war scenarios, but this time with the thought that every major nation is a likely ally. We need international cooperation in securing and regulating the transfer of the necessary ingredients and knowledge for making NBC weapons small enough to be carried by hand or motor vehicle. For the moment, stockpiles of nuclear materials in the former Soviet Union should be the center of our attention. As a threat, biological weapons cannot be far behind. We need cooperative efforts to determine who is seeking to buy as well as sell the needed material. We must make it clear that we would hold responsible and retaliate against any country implicated in such actions in support of terrorism.

At a time when we have an enormous and underutilized capacity to gather intelligence, the threat of NBC terrorism should be near the top of any list of new priorities. Every available device and every available ally must be enlisted in a continuing effort to detect any such threat, including a sharp focus on the activities of hostile states that may be supporting such efforts. We must recognize that if prevention fails, facing the threat of catastrophic violence requires negotiating strategies that are different from the adamant refusal to make concessions that we have claimed, not always truthfully, in the past. And we will need the capacity to determine quickly the plausibility of the threat.

With regard to terrorist groups using the conventional weapons of political violence—bombings, assassinations, and hostage-taking, including hijacking—the steps we should take in anticipation of a new willingness to attack on American soil are familiar ones. We must gather intelligence about likely threats. We must monitor organizations that urge political violence as a tactic and have the capacity to use it, but with an awareness that this effort will inevitably inhibit free speech and political organization at the outer borders of political discussion, and with a concern to minimize that inhibition. If the inhibition is only of speech that urges violence—now or in the not-too-distant future or in not-too-unlikely circumstances—the cost is worth bearing. Open recruiting meetings deserve less protection than private membership meetings, but in both cases monitoring by government agents or informants must be allowed wherever an organization capable of carrying out violent political action is urging supporters to consider that path.

We must exchange information with our allies about organizations that are likely to be engaged in violence. Sharing within our responsible agencies is far more important than separate credit or budget enhancements. We cannot afford to have the FBI deny the CIA information it has obtained, or the CIA to deny the FBI the information it has. The CIA can protect its sources and methods by limiting the authority of the FBI to use the information without CIA consent. The FBI can control the invasions of privacy and the risk to investigative steps that come with leaks by getting appropriate assurances from the CIA.

Intelligence-gathering is the most important form of prevention of terrorism. But it is also useful to prohibit or regulate dangerous activities, and to require record keeping, in an effort to separate terrorists from their financial support, from the equipment they need, and from their targets. The barriers to car bombs that surround every embassy do work, although less attractive targets are still exposed. Whenever reasonable expenses can provide substantial protection for highly attractive terrorist targets, we must make the expenditure. Providing additional protection for U.S. domestic flights falls in that category. Forbidding financial support of any organization that is actively involved in supporting political violence is effective and fair, whether the organization is foreign (where support is already prohibited) or domestic (where it is not) and even if the organization is also engaged in totally legitimate matters. We have to keep track of and regulate the crucial ingredients for bombs. Taggants in explosive materials make obvious sense.

Finally, we must train and be willing to use immense investigative resources to investigate any terrorist event targeting Americans at home or abroad. We must be prepared to prosecute any attack on Americans, even if it takes place abroad. We do not need a change in our present system of criminal procedure, or flagrant violations of customary international law, to do this. We have been extremely successful by simply using massive and well-trained investigative teams. The cost of changing the fundamental rules, even if it were possible within our Constitution, has proved too great in other countries. We do need far better acceptance by our allies of the need for international cooperation in providing evidence or the suspect. Threats will not accomplish that, but diplomacy can.

We will be confronted with situations where hostages have been taken or where there is a campaign of terrorist bombings like those in England and France. Terrorist demands made in these cases in exchange for withholding further harm must be resisted. We have made deals for hostages in the past, and it has not paid off. So has Israel, and it has not paid off there either. France has sought to deal for an end to bombings, and they have not ended. The risk of encouraging future attacks by the same group, or political violence by other groups, is too great to make concessions, at least if there is any real prospect of a rescue operation. To have that prospect, we must continue to maintain highly trained rescue teams under the supervision of the FBI and the Department of Defense. We must be willing to put great pressure on other nations to grant these forces access to hijacked planes or ships.

Exceptions to the general rule against concessions should be made only when it is clear that there is such a disproportion between the danger to the individuals and the demand that no likely encouragement of future terrorism by the departure from an established practice is likely to outweigh the benefit of saving lives immediately. When such exceptions are made, we must be prepared to follow concessions and the end of a terrorist threat with steps of foreign policy or of criminal justice that redress the balance of benefits and costs of engaging in terrorism—making sure that the final balance sheet for terrorists shows a plain loss.

If a hostile state is tolerating or supporting terrorist actions against U.S. citizens or interests, we must be prepared to retaliate militarily as we have done in Libya and Iraq. But such retaliation ought to depend on a very careful review of the facts and an honest and open statement of the legal standards we believe should apply. Being a superpower does not relieve us from the responsibility of justifying the use of lethal force that will, almost inevitably, kill innocent individuals. And the retaliation must be proportional and targeted to minimize the inevitable deaths or injury to innocent parties. Innocent deaths in the wrong nation are a double abomination.

Finally, we have to learn to manage public expectations. There will be terrorism. We can deal with it; we can discourage it; but we cannot end it completely any more than we can end violence for other purposes. The steps described in this book will help accomplish our dual purposes of limiting the harm to American citizens and protecting the integrity of our society and our governmental processes. But one of the great dangers of terrorism in every democracy is that it may lead, as it is often intended by the terrorists, to self-destructive actions. We must learn never to react to the limited violence of small groups by launching a crusade in which we destroy our unity as a nation or our trust in the fairness and restraint of the institutions of the U.S. government that control legitimate force.

Notes

Preface

1. Susan Sachs et al., "Zealot's History, The World Trade Center Bombings," *Newsday*, June 13, 1993, p. 7. See also Robert McFadden, "Trade Center Closer to Closure," *Orange County Register*, November 13, 1997, p. A1.

2. As quoted in Richard Bernstein: "On Trial: An Islamic Cleric Rattles Secularism," *New York Times*, January 8, 1995, section 1, p. 1.

3. Ibid.

4. Ibid.

5. Ibid.

6. Brandon Stickney, *"All-American Monster": The Unauthorized Biography of Timothy McVeigh* (New York: Prometheus Books, 1996).

7. Dale Russakoff and Serge F. Kovaleski, "An Ordinary Boy's Extraordinary Rage," *Washington Post*, July 2, 1995, section A, p. 1.

8. Stickney, *"All-American Monster"*, pp. 198–199.

9. "Militia" is the term given to the various, pseudo-military grassroots organizations scattered throughout America. In addition to community meetings and rallies, the more active militia groups are known for their military style of organization, weapons stockpiling, and the military training that they offer to their members. Although originally organized on a local basis, by 1995 several militia had begun attempts to organize on the national level. The range of political views among the militias range from libertarianism and the right to bear arms to ultra-racial supremacy. For a brief description of the various militia groups in existence at the time of the Oklahoma City bombing, see "Sketches of Militia Groups," *USA Today*, January 30, 1995, p. 7A.

10. Patrick E. Cole, "Diaries Dearest," *Time*, March 31, 1997, p. 26. Andrew Macdonald is a pseudonym for William Pierce.

Chapter 1

1. James Risen, "CIA Director Predicts Terrorism Rise," *Los Angeles Times*, December 20, 1995.

2. Alex P. Schmid and Ronald D. Crelinsten, *Western Responses to Terrorism* (London: Frank Cass, 1993), p. 11.

3. Ibid., pp. 7–13.

4. Benjamin Netanyahu, *Fighting Terrorism: How Democracies Can Defeat Domestic and International Terrorism* (New York: Farrar, Straus, and Giroux, 1995).

5. Ibid., p. 268.

6. Richard E. Nisbett and Lee Ross, *Human Inference: Strategies and Shortcomings of Social Judgement* (Englewood Cliffs, N.J.: Prentice-Hall, 1980), p. 62.

Chapter 2

1. Western democracies vary in the specifics of their regulation of intelligence agencies, but the general systems are similar. For example, for electronic surveillance within Germany, the German domestic intelligence agency, the BfV, must follow the provisions of a special statute, the so-called "G-10 Law." This requires an application for a written order from the Interior Minister explaining who is to be monitored and why. Acceptable reasons are limited to the suspected commission of certain specified criminal offenses, including formation of or support for a terrorist organization. If the Interior Minister agrees, he or she must submit the application to a special commission that possesses judicial powers. The surveillance is limited to three months. A special parliamentary board within the Bundestag must be informed of all ongoing and concluded electronic surveillance. The German BfV is generally responsible to the Federal Minister of the Interior and to a special parliamentary control commission within the Bundestag that meets secretly every three months and consists of particularly trusted members of the political parties in Parliament.

2. Don A. Schanche, "Italy Says Abbas was Freed Under Diplomatic Status," *Los Angeles Times*, October 15, 1985, part 1, p. 4.

3. Anthony O. Miller, *United Press International*, October 13, 1985, Washington News Section, Sunday AM Cycle.

4. Ibid.

5. E.J. Dionne, Jr., "President Sends Conciliatory Note to Italian Leader," *New York Times*, October 20, 1985, section 1 part 1, p. 1.

Chapter 3

1. "A Link to a Chain of Disasters," *Los Angeles Times*, September 11, 1985, Metro, part 2, p. 4.

2. For works by Dr. Merari, see Ariel Merari, ed., *On Terrorism and Combating Terrorism: Proceedings of an International Seminar* (Frederick, Md.: University Publications of America, 1985); Ariel Merari, *PLO, Core of World Terror* (Jerusalem: Carta, 1983); and Ariel Merari and Shlomi Elad, *The International Dimension of Palestinian Terrorism* (Jerusalem: Jerusalem Post, 1986).

3. Abraham Sofaer, "Fighting Terrorism Through Law," *Department of State Bulletin*, October 1985, p. 38.

4. In the spring of 1996, a dozen members of a militia group known as the Freemen barricaded themselves on a ranch 30 miles outside of Jordan, Montana. The Freemen were wanted by federal agents on charges of bank fraud, mail fraud, and threatening government officials. There was no assault on the ranch. The standoff lasted 81 days before the Freemen were peacefully taken into custody. For more information on the events at Waco, Texas and Ruby Ridge, see above, p. xviii.

5. The raid by Israeli Special Forces at Entebbe Airport in Uganda in 1976 came after Palestinian sympathizers seized an Air France jetliner carrying Israeli passengers. Under the cover of darkness the commandos attacked the terrorists, killing all seven, while one Israeli commando and twenty Ugandan troops were lost. Although three hostages were killed, 103 were saved. West Germany's 1977 rescue followed the seizure of a German Lufthansa jetliner that was then flown to Mogadishu, Somalia. West German commandos struck a little after midnight, killing three terrorists and wounding the fourth. All 86 hostages were rescued.

6. The U.S. government sold weapons to Iran in order to gain the release of American hostages held in Lebanon. The proceeds from the sale of weapons to Iran was then funneled to the Contra military forces fighting the Sandinista government in Nicaragua.

Chapter 4

1. The 1989 invasion of Panama by U.S. troops was intended to oust strongman Noriega and stabilize the country by establishing a legitimate democratic government. In order to accomplish this goal, approximately 28,000 U.S. troops were used in the invasion, 23 of whom were killed and 338 of whom were wounded. The Panamanian people suffered from the inva-

sion as well, with an estimated 500 dead and approximately $700 million in property damage. See Nathaniel Shepard Jr., "Years Later, Panama Still Aches After Invasion," *Chicago Tribune,* December 16, 1990, p. 1.

2. 494 U.S. 259 (1990).

3. 504 U.S. 655 (1992).

4. Alex P. Schmid and Ronald D. Crelinsten, *Western Responses to Terrorism* (London: Frank Cass, 1993), p. 13.

5. 18 U.S.C. 32 (1984).

6. 18 U.S.C. 1203 (1984).

7. In fact, even when the requested state is sincere in its efforts to prosecute, most terrorism cases do not result in convictions. According to German Justice Ministry official Peter Wilkitzki, between 1980 and 1985, Germany refused extradition in 69 cases, instead attempting to prosecute in its domestic courts. Not one of these prosecutions was successful, generally because Germany was unable to gather adequate evidence.

8. Case Program, John F. Kennedy School of Government, Harvard University, *Terrorism in the cour d'Assises: The U.S. v. France v. Georges Ibrahim Abdallah,* C16-89-904.0, 1989, p. 27.

9. In 1988, officials in Greece arrested Mohammad Rashid, a Palestinian who was suspected of having bombed a Pan American airliner in 1982. The plane made an emergency landing in Hawaii after the bomb was detonated in midair, killing one person and injuring fifteen. Despite repeated requests by the United States for extradition of Rashid, Greece refused to turn him over and tried Rashid for his part in the bombing in Greece.

10. 18 U.S.C. 2331 (1996).

11. Ethan Nadelmann, *Cops Across Borders: The Internationalization of U.S. Criminal Law Enforcement* (University Park: Pennsylvania State University Press, 1993) p. 201.

Chapter 5

1. Geoffrey Levitt, *Democracies Against Terror: The Western Response to State Supported Terrorism* (New York: Praeger, 1988), pp. 72–75. See also Executive Order 12538, Imports of Refined Petroleum Products From Libya, November 15, 1985; Executive Order 12543, Prohibiting Trade and Certain Transactions Involving Libya, January 7, 1986; and Executive Order 12544, Blocking Libyan Government Property in the United States or Held by U.S. Persons, January 8, 1986, in *International Terrorism: A Compilation of Major Laws, Treaties, Agreements, and Executive Documents,* prepared by the Congressional Research Service, Library of Congress, for the Committee on Foreign

Affairs, U.S. House of Representatives (Washington, D.C.: U.S. Government Printing Office, July 1991), pp. 268–270.

2. See Bruce Hoffman and Caleb Carr, "Who is Fighting Whom," *World Policy Journal*, Vol. 14, No. 1 (Spring 1997). Hoffman cites the RAND St. Andrews University Chronology of International Terrorism as claiming at least fifteen identifiable state-sponsored terrorist incidents in 1987 and eight in 1988.

3. U.S. Department of State, *Patterns of Global Terrorism, 1987*, Washington, D.C., August 1988, p. 37.

Chapter 6

1. Biological weapons are capable of reaching and infecting more victims through dispersal, and they cause effects that are more difficult to detect and occur over a longer period of time. See Ruth SoRelle, "U.S. Lacks Preparation to Battle Biological Terrorism, Expert Says," *Houston Chronicle*, March 11, 1998, section A, p. 8. This article quotes Dr. Donald A. Henderson, Professor Emeritus of Public Health at Johns Hopkins University School of Public Health, on the difference between biological and chemical weapons. See also Joseph Douglass and Neil Livingstone, *America the Vulnerable* (Lexington, Mass: Lexington Books, 1987).

2. Taggants are multi-layered particles of color-coded plastic, smaller than flakes from a pepper grinder. These particles are mixed with explosives during the manufacturing process. After a bomb is exploded, the particles can be found with a magnet or ultraviolet light and be examined under a microscope for a color sequence that identifies the explosive's manufacturer, batch number, and production date. For a brief description of taggants, see Ron Martz, "Atlanta Bombings: Looking for Answers," *Atlanta Journal/ Constitution*, March 3, 1997, p. B4. See also U.S. Department of Treasury Progress Report, *Study of Marking, Rendering Inert and Licensing of Explosive Material*, March 4, 1998; and Warren Leary, "Panel Rejects Adding Markers to Explosives," *New York Times*, March 5, 1998, section A, p. 22. The article discusses a National Research Council report casting doubt on the use of taggants. The NRC was commissioned by Congress to examine and report on taggants, and supplied the report on the same day that the Treasury Department made its progress report that found further examination was required.

3. *Loose Nukes, Nuclear Smuggling, and the Fissile-Material Problem in Russia and the NIS*, Hearing Before the Subcommittee on European Affairs of the Committee on Foreign Relations, 104th Congress, 104-253 (1995). (Statement of Professor Graham T. Allison of the Belfer Center for Science and International Affairs, Kennedy School of Government, Harvard University.)

4. John Foster, "Nuclear Weapons," *Encyclopedia Americana*, Vol. 20 (New York: The Americana Corporation, 1973), pp. 520–522.

5. Graham T. Allison, Owen R. Coté, Jr., Richard A. Falkenrath, and Steven E. Miller, *Avoiding Nuclear Anarchy: Containing the Threat of Loose Russian Nuclear Weapons and Fissile Material* (Cambridge, Mass.: The MIT Press, 1996), p. 24.

6. Ibid., p. 6.

7. This information is based upon conversations with Professor Matthew Meselson, Department of Molecular and Cellular Biology, Harvard University.

8. Sheik Abdel-Rahman first entered the United States in July 1990, despite his name being on a list of suspected terrorists using a visitor's visa from Sudan. By the time the error was detected, Abdel-Rahman had claimed political asylum and was released on his own recognizance with instructions to appear for a hearing by the INS within eighteen months. Overcrowding of detention centers used by the INS contributed to his release. Ramzi Yousef arrived in the United States six months before the World Trade Center bombing. He also sought political asylum and was released due to a lack of detention space. The INS has explained the entry of both men as due to miscommunication among Immigration officials.

9. 18 U.S.C. 2331 (1996).

10. U.S. Department of Justice, *Report on the Availability of Bomb-Making Information*, Submitted to the U.S. House of Representatives and U.S. Senate, April 1997.

11. 18 U.S.C. 1961 et seq. (1994).

12. 395 U.S. 444.

13. The effect of differences in national views on this question is dramatically illustrated by Denmark's extradition of an American neo-Nazi to Germany during the summer of 1995. Gary Lauck, a U.S. citizen, was a principal supplier of propaganda to German neo-Nazis for decades. Support for Nazi organizations is illegal in Germany, but the United States could not extradite Lauck to Germany, despite its frequent requests, because his activity was protected free speech in the United States. However, when Lauck went to a convention of neo-Nazis in Denmark, he became subject to extradition by the Danish government because his speech violated Denmark's laws against racist speech.

14. Guidelines for Coverage of Terrorist Acts, *ABC News Nightline*, sect. II.11(3). 1995.

15. 18 U.S.C. 1961 et seq. (1994).

16. Joe Brooke, "Crimes Against Muslims," *New York Times*, August 28, 1995, p. A3.

Chapter 7

1. Testimony of Louis B. Freeh, Director, FBI, Hearing of the Terrorism, Technology and Government Information Subcommittee of the Senate Judiciary Committee, 1996 Atlanta Olympic Park Bombing, July 28, 1997.

2. Christopher Hewitt, *The Effectiveness of Anti-Terrorism Policies* (Lanham, Md.: University Press of America, 1984).

3. Irwin Spitzer, "Big Spending Leads to Heist Suspects," *Patriot Ledger* (Quincy, Mass.), March 3, 1998, p. 4.

4. Erin DeYoung, "Britain Closes Police Case in Ulster Deaths," *The Washington Post*, January 26, 1988, p. A20.

5. Federal Rule of Evidence, 804(6); 1998.

6. Northern Ireland Information Service, *Statistics on the Operation of Northern Ireland Emergency Provisions Act, July–September 1996* (Belfast: Statistics and Research Branch, Criminal Justice Policy Division, Northern Ireland Office, 1996), pp. 5–6.

7. *Gerstein v. Pugh*, 420 U.S. 103 (1975); *Miranda v. Arizona*, 384 U.S. 436 (1966); *Massiah v. United States*, 377 U.S. 201 (1964).

8. *Bordenkircher v. Hayes*, 434 U.S. 357 (1978).

Chapter 8

1. David Burnham, *Above the Law: Secret Deals, Political Fixes, and Other Misadventures of the U.S. Department of Justice* (New York: Scribner, 1996), p. 135.

2. Serge Schmemann, "Israel Seeks to Justify Physical Coercion of Prisoners," *New York Times*, May 11, 1997, p. 15A.

3. U.S. Attorney General's Guidelines on General Crimes, Racketeering Enterprise and Domestic Security/Terrorism Investigations. See 32 *Criminal Law Reporter* BNA 3087, pp. 3092–3093.

4. Ibid., p. 3091.

5. Senate Report 101-46 at 2 (1989).

6. Ibid., p. 64.

7. Ibid., p. 4. The report also states that "according to FBI experts, in handling assets, one of the key elements to success is the verification of the accuracy of the information being furnished. This presents difficulties at times to the

handling Special Agent and Supervisor, especially in foreign counter-intelligence and international terrorism matters, since many times this information is not reasonably verifiable. But FBI experts say that solutions to this do exist and that the asset's information can be verified through other agencies, the use of a polygraph, or the appropriate caveat by office of origin to show that the information is not verifiable or is an analysis by the asset of publications he has obtained" (p. 68).

Chapter 9

1. For an excellent comprehensive study, see Richard A. Falkenrath, Robert D. Newman, and Bradley A. Thayer, *America's Achilles' Heel: Nuclear, Biological, and Chemical Terrorism and Covert Attack* (Cambridge, Mass.: The MIT Press, 1998).

Index

The Robert and Renée Belfer Center
for Science and International Affairs

Graham T. Allison, Director
John F. Kennedy School of Government
Harvard University
79 JFK Street, Cambridge MA 02138
(617) 495-1400

The Belfer Center for Science and International Affairs (BCSIA) is the hub of research, teaching, and training in international security affairs, environmental and resource issues, and science and technology policy at Harvard's John F. Kennedy School of Government. The Center's mission is to provide leadership in advancing policy-relevant knowledge about the most important challenges of international security and other critical issues where science, technology, and international affairs intersect.

BCSIA's leadership begins with the recognition of science and technology as driving forces transforming international affairs. The Center integrates insights of social scientists, natural scientists, technologists, and practitioners with experience in government, diplomacy, the military, and business to address these challenges. The Center pursues its mission in four complementary research programs:

• The International Security Program (ISP) addresses the most pressing threats to U.S. national interests and international security.

• The Environment and Natural Resources Program (ENRP) is the locus of Harvard's interdisciplinary research on resource and environmental problems and policy responses.

• The Science, Technology, and Public Policy (STPP) program analyzes ways in which science and technology policy influence international security, resources, environment, and development, and such cross-cutting issues as technological innovation and information infrastructure.

• The Strengthening Democratic Institutions (SDI) project catalyzes support for three great transformations in Russia, Ukraine, and the other republics of the former Soviet Union—to sustainable democracies, free market economies, and cooperative international relations.

The heart of the Center is its resident research community of more than one hundred scholars: Harvard faculty, analysts, practitioners, and each year a new, interdisciplinary group of research fellows. BCSIA sponsors frequent seminars, workshops, and conferences, many open to the public; maintains a substantial specialized library; and publishes a monograph series and discussion papers. The Center's International Security Program, directed by Steven E. Miller, publishes the BCSIA Studies in International Security and sponsors and edits the quarterly journal *International Security*.

The Center is supported by an endowment established with funds from Robert and Renée Belfer, the Ford Foundation, and Harvard University, by foundation grants, by individual gifts, and by occasional government contracts.